Towards Theory and Practice of Pastoral Counseling in Africa

European University Studies

Europäische Hochschulschriften
Publications Universitaires Européennes

Series XXVII

Asian and African Studies

Reihe XXVII   Série XXVII
Asiatische und Afrikanische Studien
Etudes asiatiques et africaines

Vol./Bd. 25

PETER LANG
Frankfurt am Main · Bern · New York · Paris

Abraham Adu Berinyuu

Towards Theory and Practice of Pastoral Counseling in Africa

PETER LANG
Frankfurt am Main · Bern · New York · Paris

CIP-Titelaufnahme der Deutschen Bibliothek

BV
4012.2
.B37
1989

Berinyuu, Abraham Adu:

Towards theory and practice of pastoral counseling in Africa /
Abraham Adu Berinyuu. - Frankfurt am Main ; Bern ; New York ;
Paris : Lang, 1989
   (European university studies : Ser. 27, Asian and African
   studies ; Vol. 25)
   ISBN 3-631-42146-X

NE: Europäische Hochschulschriften / 27

Library of Congress Cataloging-in-Publication Data

Berinyuu, Abraham Adu.
   Towards theory and practice of pastoral counseling in Africa /
Abraham Adu Berinyuu.
     p.   cm. -- (European university studies. Series XXVII,
Asian and African studies ; vol. 25 = Europäische Hochschul-
schriften. Reine XXVII, Asiatische und afrikanische Studien ;
Bd. 25)
   Includes bibliographical references.
   ISBN 3-631-42146-X

ISSN 0721-3581
ISBN 3-631-42146-X

© Verlag Peter Lang GmbH, Frankfurt am Main 1989
All rights reserved.

Printed in Germany 1 2 3 4 5 6 7

To my wife, Esther Afisah, without whose support, understanding, and patience this volume would not be possible.

To all people who have struggled and suffered through crises of various natures and have sought and found healing and guidance or continue in their search.

PREFACE

In this volume, I have attempted to do what could have been considered undesirable a decade ago. With the advent of Christianity in Africa, also came an effort to deny what constituted an African. African culture was called pagan and satanic. Almost every African practice was condemned. This attitude was even introjected by many African Christians and ministers. However, although Christ is above culture and against culture, Christ is also of culture and for culture. In other words, there is some humanness of Christ in the gospels, and denial of this makes Christ incomplete. Unfortunately, it seems the earlier missionaries and even some African Christians feel that the African can be complete if his/her culture is denied him/her.

The underlying principle of motivation in this volume is that only when the African is understood as a product of culture, can any ministry be effective and relevant. I am aware of those who want to engage in "spirit talk" and say that everything depends on the Holy Spirit. I believe that, though God's Spirit can do everything, the Spirit does not do anything that violates the respect of God's creation. Hence, in this volume I have tried to look at the African in his/her cultural milieu and have also attempted to look at ways of offering healing approaches that draw on some of these God-given resources. I know many will be disappointed by the lack of any heavy Christian theologizing. This is intentional. I present the African with his/her human liabilities and resources from which we can draw, in order to offer an authentic, relevant healing. I am aware of the limited scope of my data, but I do not apologize. I hope and pray that other Africans may take up where I have left off, or even correct any errors, and present the African "living human document" as a cultural product.

In Chapter One, pastoral counseling is critically examined from an African context.

In Chapter Two, I have looked at personality, which forms the spirituality of many Africans, and have also given an approach to an African Christian Anthropology.

In Chapter Three, I have described, analyzed, and interpreted healing from an African perspective.

In Chapter Four, I have dialogued this kind of African healing with one of the most popular, and perhaps the oldest, schools of healing - Freudian psychoanalysis.

In Chapter Five, I have attempted to further dialogue this kind of African therapy with a less popular school, but one which seems to have influenced some African psychiatrists.

In Chapter Six, I have integrated African and western forms of healing, drawing mostly from the developmental school represented by Erickson, as applied to pastoral counseling by Donald Capps.

Chapter Seven suggests the direction counseling can take in Africa, drawing from African background, translated into a conceptual framework.

Let us join together and tell the Story of Africa for it is long overdue. It is unfortunate that the world is deprived of the rich experiences of the human family which are enhanced as we discover our diversities in the global village - the cosmos. If Christ died for all because God loved all, then all must be important, be loved, love and be shared, and share.

ACKNOWLEDGEMENTS

In the course of producing this volume, I have partners whose contributions go beyond and above the call of duty and friendship.

Special thanks go to the Presbyterian Church of Ghana for her continuing nurture, encouragement and permission to study.

I am also indebted to professors Dr. James N. Lapsley, Jr. and Dr. Clarice Martin of Princeton Theological Seminary, who encouraged and supported me, along with Dr. Asante Antwi of Trinity College, Legon, Ghana.

Special thanks to Dr. Don S. Browning, Alexander Campbell Professor of Religion and Psychological Studies, The Divinity School, University of Chicago, and Dr. Owe Wikstrom of the University of Uppsala, Sweden. They all carefully read through this volume and gave me helpful ideas.

Another partner is Miss Catherine Campbell, an English teacher of Princeton, New Jersey. She painstakingly read and edited this volume.

A word of thanks to special friends - Setriekpor Nyomi, who as my ever present friend shares my burdens with me, his wife Akpene and Nunana their son, who gave me special joy and delight in his uninvited interest in rearranging my books and papers when they visited.

Special thanks to Nyambura J. Njoroge and her husband and children who gave me encouragement and friendship. Nyambura did not only tirelessly make time to read but suggested some ideas.

Robert Naah Loggah of the Christian Council of Ghana needs special thanks. His undeserving and unswerving friendship is more than I can express here.

This volume would not have been possible without the untiring efforts of Margaret Myers of Princeton, New Jersey and Barbara Williams of Indianapolis, Indiana, who carefully read, edited and typed the manuscript.

I also thank the faculty of theology of the Catholic Institute of Higher Education in East Africa, publishers of the Journal, African Christian Studies, for permission to rework chapter 3 which originally appeared as "The Practice of Divination and Pastoral Counseling in Ghana", ACS vol. 3, no. 3, Sept.,

1987.

There is one special friend for whom words are insufficient to express my heartfelt thanks. She is Esther Afisah, my wife, my friend, and my companion, who sacrificed company for loneliness in the course of producing this volume. Her inexhaustible love and patience make her more than a co-author. She is my animator. She not only loves and feeds me, but keeps me sane, human, African, and Christian.

Finally, I take responsibility for my views expressed in this volume.

TABLE OF CONTENTS

Chapter 1

An African Pastoral Counselor -- Problem of Definition

The presence of the Christian Ministry in Africa presents a number of unique problems to the people/natives of Africa. Despite the fact that it is carried out with relative success, the role of the Ministry is difficult to define. Indeed, it is even more difficult if one tries to give a definition that reflects an African sociocultural and psycho-religious perspective.

One of the reasons for this difficulty may be the multipurpose and multidimensional nature of the Christian Ministry in Africa. In Christian Ministry, there are ministries within The Ministry. There are also different perspectives in the ministry. Some of these perspectives include teaching, preaching, caring and counseling. There is no equivalent traditional role that embraces the various perspectives of the Christian Ministry in Africa. In most African communities, there are different people who perform the roles equivalent to the different perspectives of the Christian Ministry. No one individual assumes all the various aspects or areas of the Christian Ministry as perceived of the ordained minister.

The problem of definition of the Christian Ministry in Africa is closely linked to the problem of getting an appropriate category that expresses Christian Christology. Many African scholars are actively engaged in a search for an African Christological category.

There are many African communities still struggling to get an equivalent traditional title for the Christian pastor. People do not have problems calling him/her by the various functions he/she performs in the community. The problem is finding a label that reflects all those functions of a Christian Minister in Africa.

The other reason why it is difficult to define the Christian Ministry in Africa may be attributed to the connection between the Christian Ministers and the colonial administrators. In many parts of Africa, some Africans were unable to distinquish between the missionaries and the colonial administrators. In some cases, the missionaries did not give them any reason to make a distinction.

Therefore, in both pre- and post- independent Africa, some village folk often classify ministers in the same category with the other Africans who occupy political positions. In other words, some people view their ministers as members of the privileged few who have replaced the "white man."

In many respects, the lifestyles of the ministers and their close ties with political leaders, give the people cause to make such links. So it can be said that two main factors account for the problem of defining a minister in some African communities. The first factor may be what is called the internal factor which is simply the lack of the traditional equivalent of the Christian Minister. The second factor is the external factor which includes both the history of missions and colonialism and the lifestyles and attitudes of ministers themselves.

Pastoral Counseling as an aspect of the Christian Ministry is caught up in this problem. Whatever name or label is given to the minister invariably affects how people will perceive his/her ministry of counseling. Henceforth, the discussion of the Christian Ministry will proceed with reference to the minister as a pastoral counselor.

One leading African scholar, Bengt Sundkler, looked at the problem of the Christian Ministry in Africa. He attempted to relate the position of the pastor in present Africa to that of the chief in the traditional society.

According to Sundkler, the position of the chief was equated to that of the Christian Minister in Uganda. In some cases, the Christian Minister ran the Christian community like a traditional society. He writes that "it is generally recognized in Buganda that the political and ecclesiastical systems of office used to correspond very closely."[1] However, in some countries, such as Ghana and Nigeria, there was no such attempt to equate the Christian minister to the traditional chief. However, the people showed the amount of respect that was only accorded to the chief to the Christian Minister. They would take off their hats and sandals. Sundkler quotes a minister in Ghana as having said "Many do this to us because we are osofo...we do not ask for it and most times we do not even allow them to do it, but they insist on showing us their esteem and respect in the way they are used to, with regard to the chiefs."[2]

In some cases, some ministers, on retiring, became chiefs. Examples include Bishop Akinyele of

Ibadan of Nigeria and Nana Ghartey of Winneba in Ghana. In other cases, ministers became so close to chiefs, it appeared as if they were equals in the community. Indeed, in some instances, the ministers were more highly respected than the chiefs.[3]

One runs into a number of problems if the chief was adopted as an African equivalent of the Christian Minister. **(1)** It must be mentioned that not all African societies had chiefs before colonial rule, for example the Kikuyu in Kenya. In such societies, chiefs were the invention and imposition of colonial administrators.

(2) Granted that there were chiefs in some communities, the colonial administrators in their policies of the indirect rule politicized the chiefs. The effects are being felt even today in some African countries. One such effect is that an arbitrary group or family become chiefs at the expense of legitimate heirs.

As some of the chiefs were politicized by colonial administrators, they became despots or dictators. Such chiefs had/have arrogated to themselves absolute authority.

Consequently, the image of a chief as indicated above is totally at odds with the notion of a pastor as demonstrated by Jesus in the New Testament. Furthermore, the image of absolute authority may discourage anyone from approaching the chief with a pastoral problem. Therefore, the model may not be appropriate because of its liabilities to the ministry in general and pastoral counseling in particular.

In Africa, the Biblical image of the pastor as the shepherd is being used. The shepherd image emphasizes the caring and protection aspect. It may also refer to the preaching aspect of Ministry where the pastor tries to feed his/her sheep.

The image of a shepherd may be appropriately used in many ways. This will be addressed later. However, some problems with this notion of shepherd are that in some communities, it is usually teenagers who are shepherds. In other communities such as the Masai of Kenya and the Fulani of northern Nigeria, adults are shepherds.

The office of shepherd is not religious in Africa. If this symbol is used, it may exclude the religious or theological basis of the Christian Ministry.

3

The symbol of shepherd and its implication for pastoral counseling in Africa raises some concern: about the nature of counseling. One hopes that the pastor in a counseling context, does not think of the patient as helpless and sheepish, waiting for instruction and direction every moment. Though some pastors may have practiced counseling this way, it negates what pastoral counseling is all about.

The Christian community can be viewed as a new community drawn out of the larger community. Like the larger community, the new community must have an elder or group of elders to whom its members must turn when they are in difficulties. So the pastor(s) may be called the elder(s) of the new Christian communities in Africa.

Indeed, some confessional groups have some systems of Church governments that lend themselves to this type of understanding. The varied forms of the Presbyterian tradition, the Methodist class systems, and the Baptist system of Boards of Deacons are a few that come to mind. In these cases, the office of the elder in the traditional system has become a collective office in the new Christian communities.

The traditional elder or council of elders does play an effective role in dealing with crises of all types, individually and collectively in the community. One cannot help but suggest that the Presbyters, Board of Deacons, and class systems of some Christian denominations, etc. could effectively be used to enhance the role of pastoral counselors.

Unfortunately, in the church, unlike their traditional counterparts, the elders are made to feel that they are not trained and cannot counsel. In some cases when individuals and couples turn to them, some church elders resort to dogmatic rulings, arbitrations, legalistic and moralistic Christianity, and outright judgments and condemnations.

The inappropriate handling of some of these cases may be attributed to the fact that some of them forget their African traditions and try to be narrowly Christian and not African.

The irony may be that, if they go back to their homes and encounter a similar situation, they draw on their African tradition. They are then able to handle those cases at home with competence. The quality of their compassion, sensitivity, and deep sense of awareness of the dynamics and implications are

4

invariably much higher in the traditional setting.

This dilemma partly explains the author's purpose for this book. Another compelling reason is that unless African pastoral counselors study African therapeutic systems and integrate them into the Christian resources and some forms of psychology, even the Christians may not come to the church when they are in crises. They may not come because the Christian Ministry does not try to understand their world view, ethos, and "ultimate concerns."

In parts of Africa, some of the problems that used to be handled at the village level are no longer handled in the villages. They are handled in the cities and urban areas.

The majority of people may be in the Christian churches. However, the church does not seem to know how to handle some of these crises. That is not to say that the church does not have good intentions to help. Indeed they are desperately trying to help. In many of the Christian councils in Africa, there are units to deal with family life problems. The problems these units are supposed to handle range from pre-marital to marital problems.

Unfortunately, even good intentions and desperation to help may not always be sufficient to handle some problems. The church should train its staff adequately. Training needs to go beyond an ordination and/or a degree in western psychology or some equivalent.

This is not to suggest that an ordination and/or a western degree in psychology may not be helpful. However, these are only relevant if they are brought to bear on the African's understanding of herself/himself, in relation to community and the cosmos. The "human living document" must be the primary focus of whatever theology and psychology one studies from the west.

This task requires a Judgment call on the part of the African students. Judgment call means some form of criteria or methodologies that enables them to adapt, integrate, and, in some cases, reject irrelevant material.

A study of perceptions of family counseling in Nigeria showed what may be shocking results to African students of pastoral counseling. Even though this study was done in Nigeria, one would dare say it may reflect similar situations in many African countries.

Many a student of pastoral counseling seems to assume that because the problems that used to be handled in the village are now occurring and are being handled in the urban areas and cities, new approaches are needed. The assumption supposes that the old village ways do not work with people in the cities. The people who did the study in Nigeria made similar assumptions. Their assumptions were that the traditional family counseling in traditional environments had need of a review.[4]

Another assumption of the study was that "the usual kinsfolk-extended family conference is no longer a very effective couples' crisis resolution in an era of upsurge of social changes."[5]

In this study, they sent out a questionnaire that would enable them to ascertain the kind of counseling services different people with different educational levels would prefer.

The questionnaire included the following:

1) If you have a family crisis which cannot be settled between the two of you (husband and wife), who among these are you likely to take your problem to: the counselor, the pastor, your family head, your parents (parents-in-law), your intimate friend, the family meeting?

2) Do you think family counseling is likely to succeed in Nigeria? Yes or No.

3) If yes, list three reasons why you think family counseling is an acceptable service in present day Nigeria, or

4) If no, list three reasons why not.[6]

The results were as follows:[7]

If you have a family crisis... who among these are you like to take your problem to?	Counselor	Pastor	Family Head	Parent	Family Friend	Family Meeting	Total
	17	6	5	13	1	4	46
	36.96%	13.04%	10.87%	28.26%	2.17%	8.70%	100.0%

Fig. 1

The figures were broken down according to the age and educational level of participants.[8]

Couples' Choice By Age & Educational Level	Type of Help		
	Counselor	Significant Other	Total
NCE (Nigeria Certificate of Education)			
Undifferentiated	16 (34.78%)	30 (65.22%)	46
NCE and below	2 (11.12%)	16 (88.88%)	18
BA.BSC and Above	14 (50.00%)	14 (50.00%)	28
Age Groups			
20-25	2 (16.66%)	10 (83.34%)	12
26-30	5 (31.25%)	11 (68.75%)	16
31-35	2 (28.56%)	5 (71.44%)	7
36-40	4 (80.00%)	1 (20.00%)	5
41-45	2 (40.00%)	3 (60.00%)	5
46-50	2 (40.00%)	3 (60.00%)	5

Fig. 2.

The results in Fig. 1 are very startling and in many ways are making a statement. In Fig. 2, about 37% of the people surveyed will go to a western-trained counselor. Even though that is the highest figure, it is still disappointing. One would have expected that with the high degree of education and western influences, those surveyed would most prefer the western-trained counselor. The results also show that the second highest number of people prefer to go back to the family to solve their marriage problems. If one groups the family head, parents and parents-in-law, intimate family friend, and family meeting into a label called African therapy, the result will overwhelmingly indicate that people still prefer the traditional therapy. Statistically, this is translated into 23, about 49.7%.

What is also more amazing is that the pastor is least preferred. If the study is grouped into three categories thus; the western-trained counselor, the pastor, and the African therapist, the study will show that the pastor is the least preferred:

Western Trained Counselor	Pastor	African Therapy
17	6	29

Indeed, the western-trained counselor is more preferred than the pastor.

The study does provide the church in Nigeria in particular and indeed, Africa in general, with an important challenge. The challenge that the author may deduce from the study is that the least preference of the pastor does not necessarily mean people do not like the church. An important reason why the pastor is least preferred is best offered by Lartey. Although writing from a Ghanaian context, it seems appropriately applicable in Africa as a whole when Lartey suggests that "Pastoral counseling in the main line churches in Ghana appears to suffer most from the reductionism which explains away the religious experiences and expressions of the ordinary people."[9]

The author also thinks it is because the people may know that the church may be least skillful in handling family crises without resorting to condemnation.

Further, it may mean that if the church is making its ministry of healing more effective and relevant to the people she serves, she needs to integrate theology with some critically evaluated western psychologies, contextualized and integrated with the traditional forms of therapy. This approach calls for an in-depth study of African therapy and western psychologies and sound theological teaching. It is to this kind of task that the author in general has set himself. In this particular volume, African therapy is considered. As part of this task, attempts to define pastoral counseling in Africa will be made.

Two recent works from an African perspective responding to the task or challenge of the research will be examined.

In his book, Pastoral Counselling in Inter-cultural Perspective, Lartey attempts an African Cultural Values system dialogue with Gestalt and family therapy. He tries to give each side of the dialogue a fair hearing. Lartey attempts a dialogue in which each will find the other a helpful partner in healing persons in crises.

The most relevant contribution of Lartey's work for this chapter is the implication for pastoral counseling. After critically considering definitions of pastoral counseling in the West, Lartey offers one that he hopes will include "the secular and the sacred professionals and non-professionals...personal and a political thrust...verbal as well as non-verbal models of communication."[10]

With sensitivity to wholeness, Lartey offers the following definition of pastoral counseling.

Pastoral counseling refers to

> a helping activity undertaken by people who recognize a spiritual or
> religious dimension to life, which by the use of verbal or non-verbal, direct
> or indirect, literal or symbolic modes of communication, aims at preventing
> or relieving the anxieties of a person and fostering their growth as fully
> functioning human beings and the development of a society in which all
> persons can live a human life.11

Lartey prefers that the religion of people who come for counseling be taken seriously. He also believes shalom, the well-being of the person in all forms and being, should be the fundamental guide and goal in pastoral counseling.12 This he argues may be truer among the Akans and Gas of Ghana.

Pastoral counseling should also take seriously the theological, sociological, and psychological world of the patient. This should include the patients' symbolisms.13

Lartey leans on the model of pastoral counselor as an artist. Insights may helpfully enrich or benefit pastoral counseling.14

No one can fail to see the excellent attempt to integrate Christian theology, Gestalt and family therapy, and African tradition into pastoral counseling in his approach. Lartey does mention in general the world views, symbolisms, and religiosity of the Gas and Akans in Ghana. Unfortunately, he urges the model of shalom rather than asomdwee. He does not specify the types of symbols pastoral counselors can and cannot use.

While Lartey offers a beautiful definition of pastoral counseling, there is no African paradigm that, if mentioned among the Akans and Gas, would solicit the meaningful ingredients to effect Shalom, Faith, Love, and Hope. In spite of some weakness with the overall Biblical bias images, Lartey does give African counselors some valuable insights and tools to carry on the healing task.

Another African, whose works are making their way into the world of pastoral theology scholarship from an African perspective is Masamba ma Mpolo. Mpolo believes that the western form of therapy, psychiatry, and counseling have existed in Africa in different forms.15 Like Lartey, he is also of the view that

> the cultural dimension influencing individuals' concept of illness and
> behavior responses to crises, should be taken seriously so that sociology

9

and culture which play a significant role in the development of personality can become part of therapy.[16]

According to Mpolo, Africans do not need to rely on western interpretation of healing. The traditional African healers provide a modern African therapist with modes, methods, and mechanisms to evolve authentic African models of therapies.[17] The task of African pastoral care and counseling for Mpolo "is to help individuals, groups of human beings, and families to utilize the strength located in the core of their individual and group personality and culture."[18]

There is no doubt that Mpolo deserves the salute and bow of all aspiring African pastoral theologians. He has attempted to make pastoral theology more relevant to Africa.

However, in that noble task, Mpolo may be secularizing the strong religious element in African therapy by over-psychologizing. He seems to over-psychologize African religious phenomena. Hopefully, we won't repeat some of the mistakes of the west in Africa in an attempt to evolve authentic African pastoral theology, psychotherapy, and counseling.

In examining these authors one begins to appreciate the task of trying to define pastoral counseling. In an earlier article, the author suggested that

> the activities of the Christian church in Ghana, such as prayer meeting, Bible studies, religious studies for the sacraments of baptism/confirmation and other sacraments [by extension of Mbiti's definition of divining are] ways of divining, of seeking the will of God...[19]

In another article, the author also argued that "from the discussion of who and how one becomes a diviner, it is appropriate to suggest that Christian ministers/priests in Ghana can be mutatis mutandis justifiably called diviners."[20] These views are well elaborated in his book.[21]

The author does not find any reason not to stand by these positions. The following pages will explore those positions in another direction in order to effect a different emphasis. In all those works cited, the focus was pastoral care. In this volume, the focus is pastoral counseling.

In this approach, the author is taking a position of distinction between pastoral care and pastoral counseling, although they overlap. In earlier works the definition of Wayne Oates was adopted as a working one.

After a careful reflection, the author wishes to propose that pastoral counseling as a divining therapy must be based on the psychopneumatic approach. Through psychopneumatic approach, the African pastoral counseling must attempt to integrate the principles and therapeutic approaches of psychology with spirituality, both African and Christian. The African pastoral counselor uses psychological, spiritual, and psychotherapeutic models to facilitate the healing of deformations [developmental problems] and addictions and holistic growth.[22] The pastoral counselor in this approach uses both psychological and spiritual tools to help[23] persons in their growing challenges.

In the psychopneumatic approach, the spiritual dimension is as basic as the instinctive energies are to Freud and the developmental task is to Erikson. It is not an attempt

> to force upon psychology a philisophical, theological, or metaphysical
> position, but essentially we include the study of psychological facts all
> those which may be related to the higher urges within man which tend to
> make him grow towards greater realizations of his spiritual essence.[24]

In this approach both "spiritual drives" are as important and "fundamental as sexual and aggressive drives. They should not be reduced to sublimation or pathological distortion of the sexual and aggressive components of personality."[25] Even if that may be true with some neurotic cases, it is not enough reason to brand the spiritual and sexual drives as pathological.[26]

This approach further avoids the separation between secular and sacred, holy and profane, spiritual and psychological. "It does not deny that a secular psychologist or psychotherapist can be an effective agent in healing psychological deformation."[27] On the other hand, "It also acknowledges that the spiritual"[28] may be able to do the same.

The psychopneumatist may also be able to do more than both secular psychologist/psychotherapist and spiritualist each operating in his/her own discipline. The combination or synthesis must also be available for those who need it.

The notion of the pastor as a shepherd was discussed earlier. A caution was given that there is nothing implicitly religious about its background. The danger is to use it without any reference to the religious or theological basis of the pastor. The possibilities of misuse must also be noted.

11

In spite of all these problems, the notion of the pastor as a shepherd may still be an appropriate model. The author suggests that the pastor as a counselor could be designated shepherding diviner in Africa. This is an attempt to bring together two offices that can mutually enhance the Christian pastor's role as a counselor. In the next three chapters, divination as an African therapy and the diviner as an African therapist will be explored.

A pastoral counselor in Africa could be defined as shepherding diviner who **carefully guides** a **sheep** through a **soft muddy spot**.

There are aspects of this definition that need clarification.

Some qualities of a shepherd include being caring, loving and patient. The shepherd should also know the area fairly well in order not to expose the sheep to risks of such predators as wild animals and snakes, and to dangerous spots.

In like manner, the pastor as a shepherding diviner who is counseling, should be informed on the culture, on human behaviors and on the socio-cultural symbols of communication. The pastor should take seriously the reasons attributed to cultural symbols within the cultural milieu of the person to be counseled. Pastoral counseling calls for a deep sense of awareness of dynamics, their influences, and why they influence. This may also include spiritual and psychological growth through different experiences.

Carefully guide -- It is easy to wound sheep, even though sheep can be troublesome. One learns not to throw stones at them but guide them carefully. In the author's previous writings cited earlier, some analogies such as peeling palm kernel were used to describe the art of caring for people in difficulties. The same is implied here. The notion of carefully peeling is applicable to caring for sheep.

The counselor should keep helping the patient to discover insights, should challenge and motivate him/her. Even if the pastor does influence or persuade, he/she should be conscious of why he/she is trying to do that. Spiritual and psychological and socio-cultural integration are important elements in counseling in Africa.

Sheep -- A shepherd cannot be a sheep. It is only the sheep that must move like a sheep. In the same way, the pastoral counselor neither takes over being the patient nor does he/she disregard the strength, potential, and initiative for growth of the patient.

Soft muddy spot -- These soft muddy spots are dangerous for the sheep. They could get stuck. If the shepherd does not see them early, a preyer will come and destroy the sheep. Even if they are discovered, but the sheep are not guided away in time, they could develop sore feet. This could kill them or lead to some infection that could kill them.

Like sheep, humans also have soft muddy spots. These could be developmental, intrapsychical, interpersonal, moral psycho-social, and cultural or all of the above or some combination. The soft muddy spots refer to those areas of an individual that need much work to overcome a temptation, cope with a crisis, perform a developmental task, have a spiritual awakening, or psychological awareness. Counseling should aim at a holistic integration of the person as a whole person into a family and the community.

One of the important reasons why the psychopneumatic model is offered is that it may be a more workable model in Africa. The spiritual aspect of life is a reality in Africa. Beliefs in ancestors and their power to influence the living are very important to many Africans. The belief in evil spirits is another important belief among Africans.

It is not necessary to attempt to psychologize all those phenomena that are not really fully understood. As suggested by Lartey and Mpolo, the African world and Africans therein must be taken very seriously if counseling is to be effective in Africa. With a psychopneumatic approach to counseling in mind, turn to the next chapter where an attempt will be made to describe, analyze, and interpret divination as a form of African therapy.

ENDNOTES

1.   Bengt Sundkler, The Christian Ministry in Africa, (London: SCM Press, 1961), p. 52.

2.   Ibid., p. 54.

3.   Ibid., p. 55.

4.   Daisy N. Nwachukwu, "Perceptions of Family" in Masamba Ma Mpolo and Cecile De Sweener, (Eds) Families in Transition, (Geneva: WCC, 1987), p. 60.

5.   Ibid.

6.   Ibid., p. 63.

7.   Ibid., p. 64.

8.   Ibid., p. 65.

9.   Emmanuel Yartekwei Lartey, Pastoral Counselling in Inter-cultural Perspective, (Frankfurt: Peter Lang, 1987), p. 125.

10.   Ibid., p. 115.

11.   Ibid.

12.   Ibid., p. 118.

13.   Ibid., p. 122-123.

14.   Ibid., p. 124.

15.   Masamba Ma Mpolo and Wilheim Kalu, (Eds) The Risk of Growth, Pastoral Counselling in Context, (Geneva: WCC, 1985), p. 1.

16.   Ibid., p. 4.

17.   Ibid., p. 6.

18.   Ibid., p. 13.

19.   Abraham A. Berinyuu, "A Transcultural Approach to Pastoral Care of the Sick" in Africa Theological Journal, vol. 16:1, 1987, p. 64.

20.   _____, "The Practice of Divination and Christian Pastoral Care and Counselling in Ghana." in Africa Christian Studies, vol. 3:3 Sept. 1987, p. 54.

21.   _____, Pastoral Care to the Sick in Africa, (Frankfurt: Peter Lang, 1988).

22.   Bernard J. Tyrrel, Christo-therapy II, (New York: Paulist Press, 1982), p. 70.

23.   Ibid.

24. Robert Assogiolli, Psychosynthesis, (New York: Penguin Books, 1982), p. 193.

25. Robert Assogiolli, 1982, p. 194.

26. Ibid.

27. Bernard J. Tyrrel, 1982, p. 70.

28. Ibid.

Chapter 2

Study of African Personality

In this chapter, spirituality in two ethnic communities in Africa will be examined. These are the Tallensis and Akans, in the north and south of Ghana, respectively. The discussion will dwell mostly on their understanding of a person within the psychosocial and cultural milieu. However, in the course of the discussion, other examples will be drawn from other ethnic communities.

The discussion will be in four stages: **(1)** an introduction, **(2)** a description of beliefs and practices regarding person/personhood in these communities, **(3)** an evaluation of these beliefs and practices, and **(4)** a hypothesis of what could be an African Christian spirituality.

The method here is neither a comparison of Christian theology and African beliefs nor a comparative study of western psychology and some African beliefs or psychology. The purpose is to seek to understand these communities' ideas, evaluate them in the light of their newly found Christian faith, and suggest how these ideas may or may not be integrated for the purpose of pastoral care. By this approach, there is no attempt to dismiss any similarities between western and African understanding of person, or to assume any difference. The goal is to read the paradigms of the "living human documents" of these communities.

(1) Introduction

Until the turn of the century, general opinions about Africa and Africans seemed to be nothing more than some void with what appears to be moving objects. In this void dwelt the forces of evil. Indeed for some, Africa was perhaps the kingdom of Satan and all his/her followers.

These opinions may have been conditioned by exaggerated, distorted, and ignorant views of explorers, colonial administrators, and egocentrically and ethnocentrically biased anthropologists, historians, and theologians. For a majority of them, Africa had neither culture nor religion. The few who saw what might be signs of religion and culture did the common thing. They greatly distorted these to perpetuate their preconceived misconceptions about Africa. They provided their financers, both churches and government, with false but entertaining pictures of Africa. These distortions and derogatory

16

descriptions became and, perhaps today, have become a standard way of describing Africa.

The unfortunate thing was that these distortions were accepted, and desperate competitive attempts were made to find theories to justify them. One example is the book by Edwin W. Smith, the title of which is ever offensive: <u>The Religion of the Lower Races.</u> This book was part of a series to help westerners understand other religions. The aim of the series, the editors say explicitly, is "...to be impressionistic rather than educative..."[1] Smith sees the Bantus as a people to be pitied because they are less fortunate. He writes:

> In the course of this study we shall meet with much that may seem revolting because of its foolishness, cruelty and degradation, but let us go in the spirit of sympathy, [not love] remembering that we are all pupils in God's great school and that if [by], His Grace, we are in the higher class, it is not for us to despise those who are in the kindergarten.[2]

In spite of Smith's attempts to see and say some positive things about the Bantu, he was unlike Placide Temple, and too prejudiced by the popular notion of Africa and Africans of his time. He wrote, "the black man with a thin veneer of civilization and with religious faith is a dangerous person."[3] Smith like many others even thought Africans had no morals. For him "Many of the Bantu tribes were actually on the way to extinction through their beastly immorality, when the missionaries came to them."[4] Another person quoted by Smith as a well-known writer, is also further reported by Smith as saying

> The pagan African is what he is because of his religion. Give him a new religion, vital, enlightened religion, and he will be a new man. Christianity will save Him, because it will enter into every relation of his life to give it restraint and uplift.[5]

Africans may have suffered not only from misdiagnosis of diseases that they never suffered from but also from labels they were given which only showed the ignorance, insensitivity, and perhaps arrogance of people who felt they knew everything about Africa and Africans. Many of these labels included words like savage, prelogical, primitive, fetishist, and animist, to name a few. Parrinder points out correctly, not just the meaninglessness of these labels but also the degree of ambiguities associated with them. This is further complicated by the different usages employed by different so called "scholars" or "authorities" on African Religion. Parrinder was more courageous and ahead of his colleagues when he suggested that:

> it seems by far the best plan to this confusing and unjust word "fetish" [and I will add savage, primitive, prelogical] altogether, along with "juju,"... they need to be relegated to the museum of the writings of early explorers.[6]

But the ideas of Edwin Smith were some of the prevailing ideas of mission and theology in Africa. There are some basic assumptions in these ideas worth raising here. One assumption was that Africans are like empty containers to be filled by European civilization and Christianity. A later assumption was that Africans have inferior culture, mentality, and personality. According to a revised popular thought, it was possible for missionaries and colonizers to erase the entire culture, change the African thought system, ethos, and undoubtedly the belief system.

These assumptions indicate that Africa was perhaps treated with more contempt than commitment to announce the kingdom of God. Furthermore, these writers may have been not only racist but also illogical. For like all other human beings, in order to appropriate meaning from symbols, Africans need symbolic points of reference. Therefore, for these colonizers and missionaries to expect Africans to accept their symbols and faiths, without drawing on their African experience and the equivalent symbols, was not only illogical but also defied all theories of learning and human behavior.

In spite of this ignorance, the missionaries did get converts. But as suggested by K. A. Busia, these converts did not, and will not, come alone:

> The converts come with such knowledge of, beliefs and assumptions about nature, society and God as their culture offers them. These go to the root of life as well as seeking to give meaning to the whole of life, in this world and hereafter.[7]

It is legitimate to ask why the missions succeeded in Africa, considering some of the gross errors. A rather seemingly simplistic answer can be that God writes straight on our crooked lines.

While this may explain the high degree of the success of Christian mission in Africa, God also expects humans to use their talents of imagination to be co-creators with him/her. It is sheer irresponsibility and perhaps even unchristian to keep doing the wrong things with the excuse that God will correct them. The legacy of early missionary insensitivity still prevails even in our time.

Another answer could be that later generations saw the errors of the former mentality and took seriously the African cosmos and ethos. Placide Temple was among the few who recognized this problem. He also made an apt analogy worth quoting here:

> It has been often remarked that an European who has given up, during his life, all practice of the Christian religion, quickly returns to Christian viewpoint when suffering or pain raises the problem of the preservation and survival or the loss and destruction of his being ...In the same way among Bantu we see...even the Christians, return to their former ways of behavior whenever they are overtaken by moral lassitude, danger or suffering. They do so because their ancestors left them their practical solution of the great problem of humanity, the problem of life and death, of salvation or destruction.[8]

A third answer is that in spite of the fact that colonizers and missionaries presumed that Africans lacked any knowledge of nature, or of human beings, and were illogical in their thinking, their identity survived.

Thayer writes on a necessary and important component in spirituality and pastoral care which is pivotal to this discussion. "...The subject of spirituality and pastoral care must take seriously the cultural context within which pastoral care occurs. Pastoral care does not occur in a vacuum, but within a matrix of social processes."[9] It is imperative, therefore, to begin with the psychosocial and religious cultural context of Africans.

The task in this chapter may be similar to the task of pastoral theology as pointed out by James N. Lapsley for pastoral theology in general. "...The aim of such a task is grubbing in the root systems of human need and human hope with the intent to strengthen, nurture, and, if possible, to aid development that provides the particularity of pastoral theology and its potential and actual contribution to theology."[10] Hiltner also offers an instructive insight when he says, "...all realms of theological inquiry involve a relationship between Faith and Culture. Sometimes the questions raised in culture...for example, what kind of stability can man have in a world of instability...can be answered by faith."[11]

Clebsch and Jackle also observe an historical fact of pastoral care which serves as an impetus in this discussion. "Throughout its history, Christian Pastoral Care has borrowed from the societies in which it lived and has adapted to its pastoral use, various theories of the human soul."[12] Therefore, African spirituality which is particularized in a psychosocial and cultural context must be a beginning point in any

19

search for spirituality.

Personality in two Ghanaian Communities

A description of some of the salient beliefs about personality among the Tallensis and the Akans will be offered here. The description will begin with their ethos and the world view within which a person lives. Anthropologists, ethnologists, and philosophers differ in their definitions and discussions of these terms. The discussion will "dwell chiefly on the psychosocial or psychocultural aspects of African ethos, world view and person."[13]

The Tallensis and Akans are good examples because of their similarities and differences, and the extensive research done on their communities. The works of Meyer Fortes and Evans-Pritchard seem to have withstood the test of time. One of their achievements acclaimed by scholars of African culture and religion "was to bring a new dimension into the analysis of the religions of nonliterate societies."[14]

The definitions of ethos and world view offered by Clifford Geertz are working ones:

> A people's ethos is the tone, character and quality of their life, its moral and aesthetic style and mood; it is the underlying attitude toward themselves and their world that life reflects. Their world view is their picture of the way things in sheer actuality are, their concept of nature, of self, of society. It contains their most comprehensive ideas of order.[15]

Among the Tallensis and the Akans

> Religious beliefs and rituals confront and mutually confirm one another; the ethos is made intellectually reasonable by being shown to represent a way of life implied by the actual state of affairs which the world view describes.[16]

Furthermore, in these communities

> The force of religion in supporting social values rests then, on the ability of its symbols to formulate a world in which these values, as well as the forces opposing their realization, are fundamental ingredients.[17]

Only the salient issues immediately related to my subject -- Spirituality and Pastoral Counseling in Africa -- are considered. For a detailed account of the world view of the Tallensis, consult the seminal works of Meyer Fortes: The Dynamics of Clanship among the Tallensis (1945) and The Web of Kingship among the Tallensis (1949). The subject is also explored with regard to Pastoral Care in the author's first volume, Pastoral Care to the Sick in Africa.

The metaphor of the "web" employed by Fortes seems to be an accurate description of the world view of the Tallensis. The cosmos according to the Tallensis is not differentiated into secular and sacred, living and nonliving, spiritual and physical. Their world is not an either-or. It is both physical and spiritual, secular and sacred, the invisible and the visible, and more importantly, the living and the "living dead."

The spirit world is in constant interaction with the physical. Among the Tallensis, there is no festival, tree, or object that represents Naayin. The word for the Christian God or Jewish Yahweh in Tallen is derived from two words. Naa is the shortened form of Naab, which means chief. Yin is derived from a personal protector in the form of an ancestor who becomes a guardian angel for the individual from birth to death and beyond death. Hence Naayin literally means the Chief Guardian Angel. But God as Chief Guardian Angel is for everyone.

The world is likened to the web of a spider. All living (both human and otherwise) in this web have to respect themselves and each other. Both the invisible and visible dynamically interact with each other. For the Tallensis, humans are always under or surrounded by a cloud of witnesses.

The Tallensis do not speculate about a heaven. Figuratively, the world may be divided into two or three spheres: the sphere of the living, the sphere of what John Mbiti calls "living dead", otherwise called ancestor, and one above, where God dwells. The worlds of God and the "living dead" can see the physical world of the living but the living cannot see the world of God and the "living dead." The world of God is far superior. But God can see through both worlds.

The fact that ancestors are in spirit (wholly) enables them to be closer to God, for God is Spirit. The ancestors have symbolical physical representation. But they do not control God. God, according to Tallensis belief, however, has given the ancestor some limited power to influence the lives of the descendants still living. The living are in constant dependence on the "living dead" or more precisely the ancestors. Hence there must always be harmony and peace. Among the Tallensis, "society is not segmented into, for example, medicine, sociology, law, politics, and religion."[18] Ancestors play very active roles in the daily lives of the Tallensis. Meyer Fortes suggests about the Tallensis that

21

one's bond with one's lineage implies a ritual bond with one's patrilineal ancestors and other mystical forces associated with the existence and well being of the lineage. They [ancestral spirits and other spiritual beings] are the chief mystical powers governing the life of the individual.[19]

The Tallensis also believe that there are other evil spirits and beings in the world of the living whose power and effect can be destroyed by the spirits of the ancestors and Naayin (God). They therefore need to be constantly in touch with the ancestors through ritual to keep themselves protected. Hence for the Tallensis, life is a liturgy of celebration for the victories and/or sacrifices of reconciliation and/or amendments. It is within this religio-socio cultural milieu that a concept of a person or personality evolves for the Tallensis. The Tallensis, like the Dogon,

> think of a person as participating in the general condition of his society and the universe. A newly born child is only potentially a human being and must be given his [her] own sexual, social and spiritual identity by the human community into which he [she] is born.[20]

These identites are given through rituals.

The Tallensis further believe that "the ancestor spirits are the principal sanction enforcing a man's spirit to full filial status in his physical lineage."[21] The human person is at all times interacting with other beings in the universe, whom he/she is linked with by a network of relationships. The ancestors are very powerful in their daily influence of the daily life of the Tallensis. Hence, they are believed to be reincarnated, and children are named after them. People will also acknowledge their presence by giving or throwing bits of food or pouring drops of water for them when they arrive from a journey. The belief is that the ancestors are following and protecting them everywhere, every time.

The Tallensis do not have an abstract notion of a person. Whatever beliefs they have are best gathered by observing daily actions particularly at rituals. When a woman is pregnant, the Tallensis consult a diviner to determine which ancestor wants or is already reincarnated. They also consult the diviner to determine what the mother should or should not eat or wear, where she should go, whom she should see or not see, what she should avoid or do, and in some cases, even what name to give the baby. The baby to some extent is already considered unique and individual but is also considered as one who once lived.

Fortes suggests that "it is society that creates, defines, indeed imposes the distinctive signs and indices that characterize, and the moral and jural capacities and qualities that constitute the 'personne

22

morale'."[22] The person nit could also be named after a totem which symbolizes the identity of a clan. So it is not uncommon to have one named Baan meaning Crocodile, Tii meaning tree, and Kuruk meaning iron, to name a few. A psychologist like E. Goffman, quoted by Fortes, suggests that "...social organization and culture shape the expression of personhood."[23] This may be an apt analysis of the Tallensis.

Observations on ethnic communities like the Tallensis may have led sociologists like Durkheim and Maus to offer the notion of "the social source of person and self."[24] This theory was modified by G. H. Meed in an early paper ...sketch a theory... which summed up the formula "the 'I' of introspection is the self which enters into social relations with other selves."[25] In other words, it is society that informs, forms, and determines personality. But the person is not just passive. The individual is expected to appropriate what society offers into himself/herself.

These processes begin before and at birth and go beyond death. This may be a form of the life cycle among the Tallensis. "Ritual observations such as totemic avoidances are particularly significant foci for the conjunction of the internal awareness and the external expressions of personhood"[26] says Meyer Fortes.

In the belief of reincarnation, sex does not make any significant difference. Usually and not exclusively, boys are the reincarnations of male ancestors while girls are the reincarnation of female ancestors. At times, ancestors can cross sexes. In such cases, a nickname that is unisexual is used to name the offspring.

In Tallen, nit is translated as person. The equivalent in Akan is nipa. But nit could also be designated to a totemic animal. So for human being, the word is nin-voo. For the Tallensis then nit-(person)+voo-(breath) makes a person. Hence a person has nyo-vor which means literally nose-breath - life breathing. This is more than biological life, but uniquely belonging only to humans. A human being also has a sii (perhaps translated soul in English). According to the Tallensis, sii is the source of life. Sii is not identical to breath.

Sii can have an independent existence. It is believed that when one falls sick, Sii may be harmed by an evil spirit. It must also be mentioned that the Sii can be bewitched, hunted, or harmed only

23

spiritually. It is not visible to the naked eyes. The $\underline{Sii}$ can also be encountered in dreams, in prayers, and during divination. This belief about the $\underline{Sii}$ underlines why it is important to consider the spiritual dimension of a person who comes for counseling.

The concept of $\underline{Sii}$ seems paradoxical among the Tallensis. While they admit that the $\underline{Sii}$ has some independent existence, they negate the existence by the fact that $\underline{Sii}$ is still an integral part of the body until death. Indeed what really happens when death occurs is the $\underline{Sii}$ goes out of the body forever. Furthermore, while the $\underline{Sii}$ can be bewitched or harmed metaphysically, there is also a part of the $\underline{Sii}$ that cannot be destroyed. That part must always go to the ancestors. If one dies with definable cause or if somebody kills another without justifiable cause, it is the $\underline{Sii}$ that the ancestors call to inquire or answer to for being wicked. "$\underline{Sii}$ and life are closely interlocked"[27] says Fortes.

The Tallensis perceive a person as made of half the Mother and half the Father. But because they have a patrilineal or patrilocal inheritance system, most of the rites of initiation are performed by the father's side. There are, however, some rites that also involve the mother's side. For example, it is always the ancestors from one's mother's side who enable an individual to become a diviner. Fortes offers a useful summary of $\underline{Sii}$:

> The nearest thing [to $\underline{Sii}$] would be today that it is their representation and objectivation of the unity and continuity of the individual as he experiences this waking and sleeping, in his relationships with others, in his feeling about his most personal private possessions, in his image of his connection with his forebears and with his expected posterity.[28]

For the Tallensis, personhood begins in the womb and is attained gradually by stages over the whole course of an individual's life and even beyond, i.e., one becomes an ancestor. This means, one must be conceived properly according to tradition. The right rituals must be performed before and after birth. One must be born into a legitimate family, lineage, or clan. For it is these that give and shape one's identity -- the society.

Every person must be well trained in the family, lineage and clan history, heritage, fame and perhaps misfortunes, and be able to remember the names of ancestors of at least three generations. One should know the family, lineage, and clan shrines. One should know almost all one's relations both paternally and maternally. One acquires the right skills, such as hunting, cooking, and farming, in the right proportions at the right time. Finally, when one dies, the right rituals are performed in order to attain the status of an ancestor.

The Akans' belief of a person/personhood will be considered next. The Akans form large groups of ethnical communities in Ghana. They live in the Southern part of Ghana. Like the Tallensis, the definition of ethos and world view by Geertz is applicable to the Akans. Also like the Tallensis, the Akan world may be divided into three spheres: The sphere for the living (physical), the sphere for the living dead (ancestors), and the world of God. Unlike the Tallensis, the Akans have many different names for God which invariably describe what they perceive God's functions to be.

The Akans also symbolize the physical presence of God by a three- or four-folk branch of a tree called Nyame Dua, literally meaning Nyame's tree in every family house. This is a symbol of Nyame's strength and power as protector. There is normally a container of water with which the people of the house bless themselves and give thanks and praise to Nyame. He is called Nyame or Onyame (the shining one, or the glorious one as opposed to shining as Sun). Unlike the Tallensis, some of the names the Akan associate with Onyame indicate that they consider God as the Great Ancestor, Nana. There are other names which signify God's actions. For instance "oboo-adee" or Boadee", "the creator of all." He is "bore bore a boo adee" the great builder or architect. Like the Tallensis, the Akans also believe in the active presence of the ancestors in their daily lives.

The earth (Tallensis' Tengbon) and (Akans' Asaase yaa) plays an important role in their religious and agricultural lives. Fertility is associated with the earth. Indeed, the name Asaase Yaa is feminine. There are also festivals, normally celebrated during harvest, to offer sacrifices of thanks to Mother Earth. Some anthropologists have suggested that some African communities including the Akan and Tallensis, are basically earth cults. Tengbon or Asaase Yaa is responsible for a good harvest. The physical welfare of the earth, such as rains and animals' reproduction, attributes to the earth an individual life of existence that controls and regulates the life of its inhabitants. The earth is assisted by the spirits of the ancestors or the "living dead" (asamanfo in Akan, kpeenab in Tallensis). The asamanfo or kpeenab "reward harmonious living with collective prosperity, and punish strife with misfortune."[29] Like the Tallensis, the Akans also believe in the existence of destructive evil spirits who affect humans with any misfortune they can. They are evil in nature and are just there to destroy. It is the spirits of the ancestors who can stop them. The destructive evil spirits cannot be seen physically, so humans are left vulnerable. Hence, comes the need for cordial relationship with and dependence on the ancestors to take care of the living.

Like the Tallensis, every person in the Akan community must belong to an abusua (clan) headed by abusua panyin (clan head, usually the oldest person). The abusua in Akan, "acts as trustee and allocator of settlement and farm land, as judicial clearinghouse and so on."[30] This is also true for what the Tallensis call Yizug (literally head of the house).

Akans' concept of a person is similar, in many ways, to the Tallensis' but differs a little due to the fact that their inheritance is matrilineal. A person is made of mogya -- blood from the mother. The blood of the mother serves to connect the person with his/her paternal ancestors regardless of sex. This connection establishes the side of the parents the child can inherit from. It is further believed that the blood from the mother gives, at times, both the physical and mental/spiritual characteristics and even what the future of the child may be.

The man gives his life power in the form of his blood. This life power is that which gives the person his/her sunsum. The male's sunsum gives the child individual personality. In addition to personality, the male also passes on his ancestral gifts. One such gift is the spirit of Ntroro. Ntroro here seems to be the equivalent of the Tallensis' guarding spirit or patron spirit. Children are/were taught to keep the ritual of the washing of Ntroro. A sense of acknowledgement and gratitude is perhaps implicit in this. It is believed among the Akans that God delegates some power to the Ntroros. They may be considered as children of God; in other words, they derive their power from God (Nyame). They (Ntroro) intend to use their powers to protect the children of their descendants.

A person also receives from the supreme being his Okra, translated Soul, a divine indestructible life-giving force. Hence the Akans in one of their proverbs express this, "All men are God's children." At death Okra always goes back to Nyankopon, the generic name for God.

In summary, a person is made up of blood and flesh, spiritual connections from both his/her paternal and maternal ancestral spirits and a vital part from <u>Nyame</u>. Indeed one might say without the <u>Okra</u> from <u>Nyame</u>, there is no life. Nevertheless, it is important to keep these aspects of personality in balance. The cosmology, and concept of a person among the Akans is beautifully presented by Madam Yaa by Noel Q. King.[31] At death, a person goes to join the ancestors. Like the Tallensis, belief in the power and authority of spirit ancestors is best demonstrated in ritual.

Evaluation of Concepts

In both communities, there are more similarities. The differences seem to reflect mainly the inheritance system. For both the Tallensis and Akans, community is important. "Members...of a group participate in a common symbolic world that weaves together the multiplicity of threads which bind them to one another."[32] Furthermore, "...human life is a dynamic process, its activities coded and patterned in networks of interpersonal relations, forms of cultural impressions and systems of motivations".[33] The material drawn upon may have implicit ideological bias.

The first colonizers and missionaries may be accused of having superiority complexes. The African scholars and even foreigners following them may have been influenced by the spirit of African nationalism. Hence some of these scholars may have attempted to show that African belief systems were equal to western categories and in some cases the same as western categories prevailed in Africa.

By the turn of this century a new brand of African scholarship had arisen which tried to romanticize African culture. The popular phrase in Akan for this type of scholarship is "Yen san ko fa" meaning let us go back and take. That is, let us go and take up our old ways. These ideologies seem to have influenced the writing of some of the works cited.

The purpose here is to seek the meaningfulness of these beliefs for pastoral purposes. In this task, it seems one must consider the three components of a person in Tallensis: sie-soul, neug-flesh, vohom-breath, and in Akan: okra-soul, sunsum or hohom-breath, mogya-blood, as simply a duplication of a western concept. It is obvious there are difficulties associated with these categories. There is much western influence of the western trichotomy of person as consisting of soul, psyche, and flesh in these ideologies. Even western scholars do not agree on this trichotomy. It is necessary to avert the introduction of western trichotomy in Ghanaian belief of personality.

Hypothesis of Personality as Unitary

The author proposes that Ghanaians have a unitary concept of a person. In this regard I do not think Goetz's category, quoted by Shorter, is appropriate for Ghana. Goetz suggests that cosmobiology is a name given to an understanding of the place of humanity in nature which links the life cycles of human beings with the rhythms that govern the universe "...Human life reflects and extends these cosmic cycles."34

While there are occasions for some astrological events, for celebrating such seasons, Ghanaians generally do not engage in astrological science as a form of divination. Hence, Goetz's term is an inappropriate one for Ghana. The term unitary person seems to avoid dichotomy or trichotomy and even sexism.

A unitary person is a synthesis and lives with high consciousness of his/her synthesis. A unitary person is a synthesis of spiritual and physical, divine and human, finite and infinite, eternity and temporality, transcendence and immanence, natural and supernatural, sin and holiness, and of weakness and strengths.

A unitary person knows a great deal about science and nature but does not define himself/herself only in scientific and naturalistic terms, nor does he/she engage in speculations as if they were absolute determinants of his/her life. A unitary person is aware not only of his/her limited independence but also dependence on the cosmos and the powers therein for his/her survival.

Unitary persons reject total dichotomy as absolute but a synthesis of more than one. A unitary person tries to recognise all aspects of humans or personhood as attempts to serve all dimensions in any one act. Hence ritual is used in almost all activities. Survival for a unitary person in Africa is not an individualistic opportunity but includes a sense of awareness of participation in a community by all, for all, and with all.

The notion of mythical man by Ruch and Anyanwu seems to capture some of the essence of unitary person. For in both concepts, humans use myth to explain their world hence the term mythical. Ruch and Anyanwu suggest that man uses myth because

> the myth wants to satisfy all the dimensions of human existence in its concreteness. It is less concerned with knowing than with providing a feeling of security in the present, a sense of connectedness with the existence in the pasts and a permanent hope for the future.35

For Ruch and Anyanwu, mythical man or unitary person "...is a kind of steward of creation."36 Unitary person or mythical man keeps the process of creation going by ritual acts. "Thus ritual action is an integral part of the myth"[37] or at least revitalizes the unity of all his/her multidimensional nature. "There is not a domain reserved for speculative thought and another for ritual action. The thought provides the justification for the action and the action is the purpose for the thought."[38] Through the use of myth, a unitary person gives depth to his knowledge, action, and being. The use of rituals consequently gives unitary persons life-giving force and its maintenance of the unity. A unitary person avoids the dualism of Plato and abstractism of Aristotle. He/She does not succumb to the label that his/her concept expresses pantheism. For most Africans do not suggest by any means that their world is God or that God is identical with their world.

Nkrumah of Ghana made an insightful comment when he said:

> The dialectical contradiction between inside and outside [cosmos] was reduced by making the visible world continuous with the invisible world. For them heaven was not outside the world but inside it. These African societies did not accept transcendentalism, and may indeed be regarded as having synthesized the dialectical opposites outside and inside by making them continuous that is by abolishing them.[39]

The problem in this statement is that dichotomy is assumed. John Mbiti echoes similar views much better in theological language. Mbiti's writing about Africa suggests that the "invisible world is symbolized or manifested by the visible and concrete phenomena and objects of nature. The invisible world presses hard upon the visible. ...This religious universe is not an academic proposition, it is an empirical experience, which reaches its height in acts of worship."[40] God in this unitary concept is actively involved in all activities of the cosmos.

God is acknowledged, praised, and worshipped in different ways. These include sacrifices, libation, salutations. Thus, Mbiti further suggests that Africans "have no creed to recite, their creeds are within them, in their blood and in their hearts their beliefs about God are expressed through concrete concepts, attitudes and acts of worship. ...This faith is utilitarian, not purely [abstractly] spiritual, it is practical and not mystical."[41] It is mythical. A westerner, Matthew Fox, seems to rediscover a lost Christian spirituality which strengthens the African spirituality, when he says:

> Christian spirituality then, is a rootedness of being in the world. In history, time, body, matter, and society. Spirit found where (or better, here) and

not outside of these essential ingredients to human being. This means that economics and art, language and politics, education and sexuality are equally an integral part of creation spirituality ...the joy of ecstasy and shared ecstasy in celebration.42

However, Fox brings divisions as a westerner, which makes it difficult to accept his sentiments indiscriminately. So far, it may appear that for these communities, God (Nyaame, Naayin) is distant. It would appear as if God made the world, gave it to the ancestral spirits, other spirits, and humans and withdrew. Instead God is actively present.

These communities and indeed Ghanaians do not have a creed to recite on the immanence of God. The immanence of God (Nyaame, Naayin) is implied in their daily activities. This is even demonstrated by some of the names people bear. For example, Yinbe - God is present, Yinwonba - God is watching them - in Tallensis and in Akan, Nyamekye - God's gift, Adom - God's grace. The immanence of God is also evidenced in proverbs. Indeed, where the ancestral spirits are, there is God. The presence of ancestral spirits implies the presence of God. (Nyaame, Naayin)

Furthermore, in daily conversation there are expressions, verbal signs, and sighs, which are themselves prayers. The Akan will say: wo pe se wo Ka nyere kyame a, Ka kyere mframa (if you want to talk to God, talk to the air). It is common to hear short prayers of petition or praises to God such as Awurade, Naayin, Fa ma Awurade (leaving all to the Lord), Nyame Adomara (God's grace), Bun-kpeon (the powerful one).

It may be appropriate to say that the Divine Providence Concept is daily experienced by Ghanaians, so transcendence in traditional theological sense may be too abstract. Obiego makes an observation which supports this. He says that in daily greetings and response to greetings, divine providence is alluded. An invariable answer to the inquiry, How are you?, is nearly always an expression of gratitude to God, Thank God, we are well today.43 The author agrees with Obiego that invariably a prayer of petition, usually of good life, safety from sickness, and/or safety from misfortune also follows these responses.

It is this kind of spirituality that Ghanaians and indeed Africans bring to an encounter with Christian faith. In this encounter, they draw on their spirituality for their understanding of the meaning of Christ for them in the socioreligio cultural situation, and the implication of such a meaning for their lives before the encounter and after the encounter. It must be kept in mind that unlike his western counterpart, the unitary person does not have a compartmentalized world or way of life. It is not just an inward, individual "spiritual" conversion first before it affects the social and economic, etc.

For the unitary person, the whole person, and world is brought into this encounter. This may explain why there are 'family' conversions in Africa. By family conversion, one means, a conversion where the oldest decides for other members. It may sound absurd for a westerner who is conditioned to thinking in individualistic terms, whose world may be run by the rules of individualism.

The unitary encounter is a whole life, -- whole world, -- life-long process which includes both old and new experience. As suggested by Okorocha, "all of life [for a unitary person] is one inseparable whole in which God is ever immanent; this means that their conception of salvation cannot be classified as spiritual as opposed to material or vice versa."[44]

Therefore the new-found Faith

> can find hearing only by appealing to religious instincts and susceptibilities that already exist and it can reach these [instincts] taking account the traditional form in which all religious feeling is embodied, and speaking a language men accustomed to these old forms understand.[45]

In summary, there is a kind of conception of life in these communities and perhaps other communities in Africa which gives rise to what could be an African psychology. What Temple writes about the Bantu seems to be true for both Tallensis and the Akans:

> Of all the strange habits, of which we grasp neither the rhythm nor the reason, the Bantu say that they serve to acquire vigour or vital force, to live forcibly, to reinforce life, or to assure its continuity in their descendants.[46]

For the Tallensis and Akans and many African communities, Parrinder helps to express their philosophy of life or psychology of religion. He writes. "Force, power, energy, vitality, dynamism, these are the operative notions behind prayers to God, invocations of divinity, offerings to ancestors, everthing that may be termed religion."[47] As further suggested by Parrinder, the idea of force "has a determining influence on the metaphysical concept of 'being' and on the psychological understanding of personality."48 Then basic reason for all of these beliefs and practices is "to strengthen and affirm life."49 It may be safe to say that for the Bantu, the Tallensis, and Akans and perhaps many African communities. "They have a dynamic notion [of being]. ...a being is what possesses force...force is being, being is force."50

The question to ask here is, what does the unitary person want from Jesus, the Christ? The answer is meaning for life here and hereafter. It is their search for meaning that urged them to try Christ. However, the quest for meaning for a unitary person such as the Ghanaian is not an ascetic search to release the "spirit" from its prison of sin, the material body. It is not certainly an escape from a world all contaminated with sin and evil.

For a unitary person, such as the Ghanaian, salvation must include good health, prosperity in good harvest, multiplying of all the animals and birds reared, and long life -- the opportunity to live to be a sage is the prayer of many Ghanaians. This includes peace in all aspects of life and with everyone and everything including plants, animals, and mother earth; it requires an order within society. Salvation for Ghanaians is best described by the Hebrew Shalom.

Many theologians have attempted to interpret the meaning of salvation for Africans in christological terms. These include the notion of Jesus as senior brother asssociated with Henry Sawyer, as ancestor and witch doctor by Aylward Shorter, and many other such paradigms. These theological paradigms have their strengths and weaknesses for unitary persons who encounter the Christian faith. The author does not intend to respond to the need by a christological paradigm. The response emphasizes the works and functions of Christ in a pastoral direction. That does not mean to suggest that the other paradigms do not have pastoral implications. The task here is not to engage in academic questions such as the two natures of Jesus.

One alternative to this direction was given by Placide Temple. He certainly sensed the unitary and power concept and attempted to make a conscious philosophy of life around it. He developed his ideas from the Bantu perspective, which in some aspects is similar to both the Akans and Tallensis in Ghana.

He called the unitary way of life among the Bantus Jamaa, from Swahili, meaning family. He experienced this Jamaa from three basic concerns of the Bantu way of life. These are quoted by Aylward Shorter as "desire for life, the desire for security and the desire for vital union with the sources of a stronger and fuller life."[51] Hence Jamaa would create according to Shorter, a "spiritual friendship and spiritual community"[52] in which Christ is the new Adam, calling all into union. Temple did attempt to build communities by winning people to this idea. Unfortunately, it was short-lived for different reasons.

While one can admire Temple's attempt, it seems he was exporting a new form of the church. Indeed, he seemed to offer a religious community, such as those developed by the Franciscans or Maryknoll fathers, to name a few. Unlike western religious communities, one does not join an African community by choice. One is born into it. Community for most Africans is not an aggregate of individuals who consciously decide that they want or do not want to belong. Community is basically made of people with blood connection, not ideological interest. This may partly explain why Jamaa was short-lived. Perhaps the model base communities in Latin America may have been envisioned here. Temple however, leaves out, unfortunately, the power concept of life which he aptly identified.

Divination as a kind of African therapy presupposes this kind of spirituality. A personality in an African perspective does embody this form of spirituality. Consequently, any effective pastoral counseling in Africa should take this spirituality into consideration. With this as a necessary background, an attempt will be made in the chapters that follow to discuss divination as an African kind of therapy.

34

ENDNOTES

1.   Edwin W. Smith, <u>The Religion of the Lower Races</u>, (New York: the MacMillan Co. 1923), p. vii.

2.   Ibid., p. 8.

3.   Ibid., p. 69.

4.   Ibid., p. 70.

5.   Ibid., p. 71.

6.   Geoffrey Parrinder, <u>West African Religion</u>, (London: Epworth Press, 1949), p. 14.

7.   K. A. Busia, "Has the Christian Faith Been Adequately Presented?" in <u>International Review of Mission</u>, vol. 50, 1961, p. 87.

8.   Placide Temple, <u>Bantu Philosophy</u>, translated by A. Rubbens, (Paris: Presence Africane, 1959), p. 17-18.

9.   Nelson S. T. Thayer, <u>Spirituality and Pastoral Care</u>, (Philadelphia: Fortress Press, 1985), p. 15.

10.   James N. Lapsley, "Practical Theology and Pastoral Care; an Essay in Pastoral Theology", in Don Browning (ed) <u>Practical Theology</u>, (San Francisco: Harper and Row, 1983), p. 16.

11.   Seward Hiltner, <u>Preface to Pastoral Theology</u>, (Nashville: Abingdon Press, 1985), p. 22.

12.   William A. Clebsch and Charles R. Jaekle, <u>Pastoral Care In Historical Perspective</u>, (Englewood Cliffs, N.J.: Prentice-Hall, 1964), p. 76.

13.   Abraham A. Berinyuu, <u>Pastoral Care to the Sick in Africa</u>, (Frankfurt: Peter Lang, 1988), p. 5.

14.   Jack Goody, Introduction in Meyer Fortes, Robin Horton (eds) <u>Oedipus and Job in West Africa</u>, (Cambridge: Cambridge University Press, 1954), p. vii.

15.   Clifford Geertz, <u>The Interpretation of Cultures</u>, (New York: Basic Books Inc., 1973), p. 127.

16.   Ibid.

17.   Ibid., p. 131.

18.   Berinyuu, p. 6.

19.   Meyer Fortes, <u>The Web of Clanship Among the Tallensis.</u> (London: Oxford University Press, 1949), p. 38.

20.   Benjamin Ray, <u>African Religions</u>, (Englewood: Prentice-Hall Inc., 1976), p. 133.

21.   Fortes, (1949), p. 28.

22.   Ibid., p. 28.

23.   Ibid., p. 250.

24.   Ibid.

25.   G. H. Mead, "The Social Self", Journal of Philosophy Psychology and Scientific Method, vol. 10, 1913, p. 374-380.

26.   Fortes, p. 251.

27.   Ibid., p. 268.

28.   Ibid.

29.   Meyer Fortes and Robin Horton, Oedipus and Job in West Africa, (London: Cambridge University Press, 1983), p. 67.

30.   Ibid., p. 64.

31.   Noel Q. King, African Cosmos: An Introduction to Religion in Africa, (Belmont: Wadsworth Publishing Co. ,1986).

32.   Gibson Winter, Liberating Creation: Foundations of Religious Social Ethics, (New York: Cross Road, 1981), p. 30.

33.   Ibid., p. 54.

34.   Aylward Shorter, African Christian Spirituality, (London: Geoffrey Chapman, 1978), p. 10.

35.   E. A. Ruch and K. C. Anyanwu, African Philosophy, (Rome: Catholic Book Agency -- Officium Libri Catholici, 1984), p. 107.

36.   Ibid., p. 108.

37.   Ibid.

38.   Ibid.

39.   Kwame Nkrumah, Conscienism: Philosophy and Ideology for Decolonization and Development with Particular Reference to African Revolution, (London: Publisher unknown, 1964), p. 12.

40.   John Mbiti, African Religion and Philosophy, (London: Oxford University Press, 1969), p. 57.

41.   Ibid., p. 67.

42.   Matthew Fox (ed), Western Spirituality Historical Roots and Ecumenical Routes, (Notre Dame: Fides Claretian, 1979), p. 12.

43.   Cosmas O Keche Kuo Obiego, <u>African Image of Ultimate Reality</u>, (Frankfurt: Peter Lang, 1984), p. 139.

44.   Cyril C. Okorocha, <u>The Meaning of Religious Conversion In Africa</u>, (Avebury: Gower Publishing Co. ,1987), p. 48.

45.   W. Robertson Smith, <u>The Religion of the Semites</u>, (New York: 1957), p. 2.

46.   Placide Temple, <u>La Philosophie Bantoue</u>, (Paris: Presence Africain, 1948), p. 27.

47.   Parrinder, (1949), p. 8.

48.   Ibid., p. 9.

49.   Ibid., p. 8.

50.   Temple, <u>La Philosophie Bantoue</u>, p. 31-32.

51.   Aylward Shorter, "Recent Development in African Spirituality" in Edward Fashole-Luke, Richard Grey, Adrian Hasting, Edwin Tasie, <u>Christianity in Independent Africa</u>, (Bloomington: Indiana University, 1978).

52.   Ibid., p. 539.

OTHER WORKS CONSULTED

Pierre Erny, <u>The Child and its Environment in Black Africa</u>, Translated, abridged and adapted by G. J. Wanjohl, Nairobi, Oxford University Press, 1981.

Sigmund Freud, <u>Character and Culture</u>, New York: MacMillan Pub. Co. 1963.

Kwame GyeKye, <u>An Essay on African Philosophical Thought</u>, Cambridge: Cambridge University Press, 1987.

J. O. Kayode, <u>Understanding African Traditional Religion</u>, Ike-Ife Nigeria: University of Ife Press, 1984.

Eva L. R. Meyerourtz, <u>The Akan of Ghana</u>, London: Faber and Faber Ltd., 1958.

Bronislaw Malinowski, <u>Magic Science and Religion and Other Essays</u>, Glencoe: The Free Press, 1948.

Emefie Ikenge Metuh, <u>African Religions in Western Conceptual Schemes: The Problem of Interpretation</u>. Gabe Pastoral Institute, 1985.

G. Parrinder, <u>West African Psychology</u>, London: Lutherworth Press, 1951.

Kwasi Wiredu, <u>Philosophy and An African Culture</u>, Cambridge: Cambridge University Press, 1980.

E. E. Evans-Pritchard, <u>Theories of Primitive Religion</u>, Oxford: Clarendon Press, 1965.

Anthony F. C. Wallace, <u>Culture and Personality</u>, New York: Random House, 1961/70.

Chapter 3

Divination as a Kind of African
Therapy in Dialogue with Psychoanalysis

Divination is an ancient practice. The culture of the Bible also involved a form of divination. There are several instances in the Bible where divination was used, such as the casting of lots. In some cases it was used as a way of judging the victim or the innocent. It is a common practice in other cultures as well.

In this chapter divination in Africa and its relevance to pastoral counseling will be discussed. The practice of divination in Africa, as a whole, has much to offer to enhance the skills of all persons in the church who are engaged in counseling.

The traditional approaches of handling crises in Africa, as in any other culture in the world, even in highly technological societies, is to answer the immediate question of "why?"; however, that is where the similarities to other cultures may end.

Most Africans, traditionally, would initially try to diagnose by reference to common causes and cures. When a crisis persists, they have no choice but to be suspicious that there are deeper causes, hence deeper cures.

They then proceed to the diviner as diagnostician. By definition, a diviner is a person who discloses the causes of misfortune and death. His job is not necesarily to foretell the future, but rather

> to scrutinize the past in order to identify the spiritual and human agents responsible for personal misfortunes. Since all human problems, such as infertility, illness,...are ascribed to moral conflicts within the human community, the diviner's task is to disclose acts of immorality which have provoked the vengeance of the ancestors and to reveal the destructive hand of witches and sorcerers.[1]

The notion of, or process of, divination is very important because of its prominence and role in the diagnosis and treatment in Africa as a whole. Sow, Mendonsa, and Turner in their discussions of divination make invaluable contributions to the healing process. Sow's discussion will be considered first. Sow writes:

> In the realm of the traditional African diagnostician's operation and procedures, divination is an important, though not an exclusive, facet of his profession. So if we hope to understand the meaning of concepts

38

concerning sickness, it seems essential we try to grasp, at least in terms of their basic principles, not only the concrete operational modalities of divination but also the conceptual associations of such practices within the coherent universe of thought to which they belong.[2]

What is of interest is the relationship between the diagnostic divination and mentality of those who consult diviners. It is the aim of this author to explore ways of enhancing the contribution of cultural awareness-- the rich social, psychological, and spiritual dimensions--to pastoral counseling.

The discussion on divination will include the following: a) who becomes a diviner and how, b) types of divination, and c) the actual mechanics or dynamics of divination.

a) Who and How One Becomes a Diviner

In some ethnic communities in Ghana, anyone who, in his/her family or clan, either maternally or paternally, has ever had a diviner, can become one. In other words, it is partly inherited, but not through the genes. However, it is not everyone who can become a diviner just because an individual's family or clan has/had one or more diviners. One must always be chosen. The spirit of the ancestor who was a diviner must choose the individual.

There are normally signs in the potential diviner's behavior indicating that something unusual has changed in his/her life. The sign may differ from community to community. It may range from severe psychotic behaviors to a mild change of mood with no change in lifestyle at all. When this calling is recognized, tested, and confirmed by the community, the diviner-to-be goes into training.

The length, content, and symbols of training differ according to the psychocultural setting of the candidate. Like the Yorubas of Nigeria, the Tallensis of Northern Ghana, and the Ndembu of Zambia, the candidates "learn a prodigious amount of technical and oral knowledge,"[3] and learn to recite some incantations and rituals. The most important part of the training is learning to submit to the spirit of the ancestor for direction, i.e., messages, meanings, and personal formation. In divination, the fundamental assumption is that the spirits of the ancestors of consultee and diviner concerned are inspiring the diviner and are communicating with him/her in the process. However, the diviner is not always in a trance. A diviner is not necessarily knowledgeable in herbs, hence, may not be a "medical" healer. One type of knowledge is not necessarily a prerequisite for the other. However, there are people who have

39

knowledge of both. The duration of training varies according to one's previous experience and/or spiritual awareness before being called. It should be noted that one's excellence does not necessarily depend on the duration of training. One never fully graduates but always is considered a trainee in the "spiritual" matters in practice. One cardinal rule must always be observed by all: Upright living must be observed in all its broadest meaning and implications. Generally one must be above twenty years of age before being initiated with an elaborate ritual involving the community of the dead and the living.

b) Types of Divination

Sow's view is that the many forms and types of divination can be classified under two headings: inspired divination and deductive divination.

Adopting the definition of Sow, inspired divination includes "all techniques of so-called possession, aimed ultimately at plumbing the deeper psychic layers of professional adepts, adepts in states of trance induced and directed by a master."[4]

Deductive divination is the objective use of a material vehicle and

> The diviner's task consists more narrowly, in terms of operations and interpretations, of examining the evidence (series of mantic configurations) and drawing conclusions therefrom, adhering rigorously to the internal logic and laws of the science of divination.
> It is a form of diagnostic or prophylactic counsel that anyone can seek at will, aimed at establishing a diagnosis or prognosis when a decision looms or illness strikes, this type of active divination interprets real events by analyzing the configurations of objects arranged by aleatory procedures or by reading ideographic or pictographic signs; it seeks to decipher the universe as if it were a question of a text in which one would find the order of the world inscribed, a tablet on which the gods would have traced out men's [women's] destinies.[5]

Sow, in describing the functions of the diviner, seems to be echoing Antoni Boison's notion of studying the "human living document." Although one person under a given circumstance may exhibit either of these two ways, divination as deductive will be considered.

c) Mechanics or Dynamics of Divination

When a misfortune befalls someone, and the family/clan cannot determine a cause immediately, they assemble the elders, discuss the matter, and decide which diviner to consult; then they turn the task over to the diviner. The diviner's challenge is to help the family identify the

> fundamental conflict that has caused the patient to be personally afflicted with one disorder or another under certain specific circumstances.6

Sow describes the tools of the diviner as

> all observable phenomena, relating to terrestrial or elestial elements, animal or human, physiological or psychological, animate or inanimate, [which] can serve as signs [or] the moon, sun, stars, rain, of the earth, sand, stones, shells (coweries), the use of vegetable matter, seeds, nuts, the use of animals, the use of such objects as knucklebones, dice, sticks, the use of the human body, with reference to facial features, etc.7

On the subject of the mechanics or processes used, Sow continues:

> The divining process consists of three stages one after the other. These stages must come up with a diagnosis. This diagnosis in many cases is a holistic interpretation.8

> i) The first stage is the manic examination. This consists of detailed questioning of the different relational poles that form the very foundation of the patient's psychological makeup as a person.9

> This form of questioning is in pairs of opposites stability against instability, favourable against unfavourable.10

> The elements for questions are from the socio-cosmic universe which make up roots of the enquirer. They also serve to be the means by which the conflict (affliction) seeks to uproot the victim from.11

> ii) The second stage is to determine the meaning of all those symbols and signs and how formula will be arrived at that will alleviate or avert its consequences.12

> iii) The third stage is the prescription of the methods of treatment which will inevitably initiate the therapeutic procedure.13

Sow makes an adept analysis of divination. He writes:

> In essence it will consist of bringing to light the unapparent, hidden elements that make up the conflict structure reflected in the clinical case, for mental as well as organic disorders and even in a general way, for unhappy experiences, including the failures encountered in everyday life.14

Sow further makes an observation which partially undergirds the intent of this chapter. He writes:

> In this sense, divination practised,...[by] analysing and interpreting and important social concern differs in no way, in terms of the substance and nature of the diviner's role, from the activity of highly placed technocrats,

41

manipulating mathematical models on the basis of data and weighing risks, intermediate or long-term, to make their forecasts and offer advice.[15]

The method is appropriate, but the direct comparison of human problems to mathematical models on the basis of data, or equating a diviner with a technocrat, does not seem valid.

Appiah-Kubi gives an example worth quoting which emphasizes the role of the diviners in Ghana in spite of the degree of western and/or Christian influence in Ghana:

> Akosua and Ama are two close friends. Ama is married. Akosua is not. Unfortunately, Ama's husband started to flirt with Akosua, which resulted in pregnancy. During labour she became very hysterical. Not any amount of pain relievers could help her. The western-trained doctors diagnosed her as a mental patient with psychosis and asked that she be sent to a mental hospital. Akosua only got worse at the mental hospital. The relatives took her out of the hospital for traditional treatment. Through divination, Akosua admitted her sin and guilt and was made to confess. Ama forgave her. Both of their families shared in a meal. Akosua was purified of her pollution, and peace was made between the two friends and their families. Akosua is now back to normal.[16]

As a kind of analysis Appiah-Kubi writes:

> It is impossible to determine exactly how such an approach to treatment works--as it does, in case after case but unquestionably the fact that it attacks underlying problems, not merely symptoms, is carried out in a meaningful context, and is based on shared beliefs helps to explain its success.[17]

Mendonsa suggests that divination helps the Sisalas to act towards each other within their cosmos. These interactions with each other may help in partly understanding their behavior. These interactions help"persons influence, create and change the social order."[18]

Among the Sisalas, "divination provides an institutionalized technique that enables persons to do this when conflicts and disputes arise."[19] Hence divination may be helpful in offering psychological insights and social functions as well as a process "that allows participants to negotiate solutions to problems. It is a way of working out answers to complicated situations."[20]

The diviner is an indispensable figure in the tradition of the Sisala community. The Sisala people, like any primary culture, have many plagues to combat. These range from simple malaria to heart attacks. Hence, there is need for a mechanism such as divination to help them to understand and fight these misfortunes, relieve the strains and stresses of life, and keep the community together.

Research carried out by Mendonsa on why and the number of times people consulted a diviner in a given month indicates how fundamental divination is for the Sisalas:

"Number of Times Interviewee Consulted a Diviner in Previous Month."[21]

No. of Times Consulted Diviner	0	1	2	3	4	5	6	7	8	9+	Total
No. of People	37	71	90	36	22	6	3	2	1	3	271
Percent	14	26	34	13	8	2	1	1	0	1	100

Fig. 1

Reasons for Consulting a Diviner.[22]

Reason	No. of Clients	%
1. To find out about a journey	32	12
2. A matter of marriage	38	12
3. A child naming	4	1
4. An illness	102	38
5. Insomnia	12	4
6. Childbirth	18	8
7. Dreams bothering client	3	1
8. Wife's infertility	7	3
9. A death occurred	3	1
10. To learn about something in the future	3	1
11. Conflict occurring in the lineage	4	1
12. Some animals died	1	0
13. Wanted to know outcome of harvest	1	0
14. General trouble	10	4
15. No response to question	25	9
16. Other responses	13	3
TOTAL	271	100

Fig. 2

From these figures, it seems health-related problems appear to be a major reason why some of the Sisalas consult a diviner. These health-related problems, in most cases, would seem to be psychosomatic in nature.

It seems Francis may be helpful when she says, "Cultural factors and patient beliefs have been shown to influence the outcome of medical visits to varying degrees. It has also been found that personalty and social influences determine response to medical advice."[23] It may be in a case such as Akosua and Ama, referred to earlier, that the view of Mendonsa on divination may be relevant. He writes:

> Divination is a set of standardized techniques and categories of possibilities which enables clients to pinpoint the cause of action by which he is supposed to be able to alleviate misfortune. Whereas medicine is thought to work directly to remove illness, divination establishes a link with a behavioral cause of illness.[24]

There is implicit in this understanding of divination, a notion that social and personal problems, misfortunes, and crises can be translated into biomedical problems. Turner, writing on divination among the Ndembu in Zambia, echoes similar views thus: "...they (diviners)...interpret their divinatory symbols, reveal deep insight both into the structure of their own society and also into human nature."[25]

Diviners attempt to unveil the veiled hurts in the individual and the community as a whole. According to Turner, the diviner claims to try to make the issue(s) at stake as clear as possible, no matter how their clients may try to conceal and deceive the diviner. Therefore "the divinatory process consists of first bringing matter hidden to the diviner, then matters hidden to client, to light."[26] It may be when matters come to light in the client, the diviner may also understand or at least learn of them. What Mendonsa discussed about the Sisalas divination seems to be similar to Turner's discussion of the same among the Ndembu. For the Ndembu, divination "becomes a form of social analysis, in the course of hidden conflicts between persons' unconscious impulses [within persons] and factions are brought to light, so that they may be dealt with by traditional and institutionalized procedures."[27]

Insights into the Dynamics of Divination

From the aforesaid, divination is a complex phenomenon in most African communities. Its activities cover and influence wide spectra of the communities. It deals with both the individual and the community which are integrally inseparable. The role of the diviner is also inseparable from the daily lives of the individual and the community. He/She may be called a therapist, as suggested by Sow. The diviner/therapist functions by relating his duty to and drawing from the anthropological, sociological, and psycho-religious framework of the society. As a therapist, he/she seeks to integrate or strengthen his/her patients' personalities as well as integrate that individual into the family and society as a whole. Divination, as briefly described, has its basic assumptions, and operates according to a certain logic with rules and regulations. It could be said that it is a science of its own category. Perhaps it is a form of what is known as psychotherapy in the West. It shall henceforth be referred to as an African therapy. By this suggestion, one immediately evokes many questions on psychotherapy, and more importantly which school of psychotherapy. Divination as a form of African therapy will be compared with Freudian psychoanalysis.

For the moment let us go back to further exploration of some of the basic principles of this kind of African therapy. One important function of an African therapist then is to identify the conflicts within a community, their cause, and course and to suggest ways of dealing with them to bring order, stability, prosperity, and peace to the community and the individuals therein.

Divination as a form of therapy in some African communities does not always aim to heal conflict. For example, a prince may seek the service of the diviner for political reasons. It is this use of it which has led scholars like Mendonsa to conclude that divination is a form of social control over the deviants of the political or social hierarchy. This notion is alluded to by the title of his book, The Politics of Divination. Such a view is misleading because it ignores the difference between the general use of phenomenon and the misuse or perhaps another use by a few. He probably comes to this conclusion by the fact that, invariably, the elderly are actively involved in divination. However, the fact that the elderly invariably seek the therapy on behalf of the family or even an individual in the family does not exempt the elderly from being pointed out as the cause of the conflict.

African therapy "arrives at conclusions by considering elements that take into account the past and the present as well as the future."[28]

The symptoms that warn many communities in Africa of a potential conflict include sicknesses, especially sudden and severe ones, misfortunes such as accidents, and of course deaths. These symptoms cause them to go to the therapist to help them trace the course and cause of the conflict, and

45

to address it as soon as possible. Zahan prefers to call a deductive diviner as an interpreter diviner. According to him, "the interpreter diviners employ '...divinatory objects which permit them to exercise the intuition and clairvoyance and with whose aid they establish the augual theme according to the needs of their clients.'"[29] This description seems to fit Sow's in the earlier pages.

As indicated earlier, this form of therapy operates according to some rules. The tools such as the goatskin, the wooden wand, the pieces of calabash, and the cola nuts are integrally cultural symbols that only have meaning within their cultural contexts. Hence for an outsider, it is difficult if not impossible to understand the use of these objects for uncovering hidden conflicts. As suggested by Zahan, "this material is endowed by augural science with a specific and conventional meaning in relation to the signified elements."[30] These objects become the intermediary between therapist and the reality of the dynamics that gave birth to the conflict. Perhaps, he may be role-playing the initial drama with objects.

An important aspect of this therapy is the role of the ancestors. It is communication with the spirits of the ancestors that helps the therapist to identify the social web of relationship. However, it is not his duty to identify the conflict; his is to point out a conflict and allow the consultee to reflect and make the connections. The therapist may understand the conflict in general but it is the client who understands it specifically. Invariably, divination must end up with a recommendation of a kind of ritual of sacrifice that will resolve the conflict by removing the anger of the ancestors and uniting all family members together. As to how this kind of therapy ever succeeds, a suggestion by Ackernecht may be instructive:

> The therapeutic achievements of psychogenic movement do not necessarily depend upon real aetiological knowledge of casual treatment...it is quite possible that the therapeutic successes are due to the same two basic mechanisms of confession and suggestion which are so little understood and which had been used with such success by the medicine man.[31]

This point wil be taken up later, when persuasion and healing are discussed.

Another suggestion on the role of the ancestors is offered by Gluckman from a sociological perspective. For him there is competition for prosperity among members of the community. There is also competition between the individual prosperity and the community prosperity. So they set up a moral order in which individuals can work, marry, and take care of their families. The political moral order "becomes invested with occult values which hide the potential conflict between communal well-being and well-being for all individuals. These values are expressed in beliefs and rituals."[32] Although a sociological insight will be used later, the observations by Gluckman are not so appropriate here. Gluckman does not seem to understand the significance of the political moral order in most African societies. If anything, the political moral order addresses the individual and communal conflicts very constructively. The individual and the society are not necessarily always against each other. The political moral order prevents the community and social solidarity from breaking into chaos.

Gluckman draws conclusions inappropriately from the works of Fortes and Evans-Pritchard. He also makes a comparison between an African village and a family firm in industrial England, where members "are worker-shareholders and competitors for executive positions."[33] So he draws the conclusions based on his understanding of an African village or community in a capitalistic category and sees conflicts similar to those found in industry. This kind of analysis seems to be a typical example of some western scholars who were and are desperate to find ways of fitting other cultures into western cultural systems. The fact is that in most African communities, there are centuries of traditions of how a family runs. There is a place guaranteed for every member. The basic principle of an African community is interdependence. The strength of the community depends on the degree of solidarity. Economics may be the tool to that end but never a means to destroy the community. So his comparisons do not seem to be appropriate.

Another value of divination may be that the culprit personally or the victim on behalf of someone's conflict is not left alone to face the problem, nor is the victim just blamed in order to induce guilt and shame. There is community sharing of the guilt or shame. The purpose is to reintegrate the individual back to himself/herself, the community, and the cosmos. In addition to whatever medical treatment is given, this kind of African therapy heals the psychological and/or psychosomatic aspects of the conflict. This could account for its relative success over the centuries.

As indicated earlier, the ancestors play an important role in African therapy. Some attempts have been made to give a psychological interpretation of the belief in ancestors and their role in life as a whole. A few of these psychological interpretations will be briefly surveyed here.

47

Goody suggests that African life embraces all aspects of life and that "they [Africans] worship their ancestors because ancestry, more particularly parenthood, is the critical and irreducible determinant of their whole social structure."[34] Horton builds on these and further suggests that "...these notions constitute indigenous social psychologies."[35] By this he means "a way of explaining, predicting and attempting to control the relationship between the individual and his or her society."[36] For Fortes, the definition of a person is inseparably tied with his/her ancestors. So the belief in, or concept of, ancestors "is the religious counterpart of their social order, ...investing it with value that transcends mundane interest and providing for them the categories of thought and belief by means of which they direct and interpret their lives and actions."[37] The implication of Fortes' view could be that African therapy for real life situations is projected out there to ancestors. This notion will be discussed in detail in the next chapter. However, a danger in the view could be that, when stretched to its logical conclusion, one may negate the possibility that there are some supernatural influences in African therapy that help Africans to deal with their conflicts.

Another view on the concept of ancestor worship is that it "is an institutionalized scheme of beliefs and practices by means of which men can accept some kind of responsibility for what happens to them and yet feel free of blame for failure to control the vicissitudes of life."[38] The implication of this view of African therapy may be that the individual is free to express anger, guilt, and shame, yet take no responsibility. He/she is both the victim and the victor.

Furthermore, the belief or concept of ancestor is compared to the Oedipus and Job paradigms. The Oedipus and Job paradigms have been dealt with in detail by Freud.

In Oedipus, the victim or the one who causes sin neither feels guilt or shame nor does he/she take responsibility for his/her actions. The sin or act that gave birth to the conflict is seen as an unavoidable circumstance to the victim. It is an external imposition; the individual cannot do otherwise. This paradigm does not seem to reflect, in any way, what most African communities believe about themselves and the ancestors. The rituals which normally follow therapy invariably are aimed at accepting guilt/blame/shame, taking responsibility, and even, in some cases, restitution.

48

The Job paradigm is more or less the opposite of the Oedipus. Job's paradigm neither attempts to suggest outside influences from which he cannot do anything nor is it necessary he understand from where they come. Instead, the rewards and punishments are given by God who does not act arbitrarily but in a covenant relation with humans. Job thought he would win God's favor by being responsible in this covenant relationship. Instead, he is rewarded with misery and suffering.

The lesson for Job is that he is not an equal with God. No superior responsible acts can win God's favor. Job simply admits guilt for his actions. "He accepts his total dependence on the all-omnipotent power of God and puts himself under God's control without question. God for Job is an all-powerful father figure, from whom his life depends."[39]

The implication of this paradigm for African therapy may be two-fold. First, once they obey the authority of the father figures embodied in moral codes, and memories of father figures, there are no conflicts. It is only when they begin to assert their own individuality that conflicts arise. The purpose of therapy then is to help them remain under the authority or the power of the ancestor or some otherwise projected authority in their midst embodied in moral codes. This may be true in some cases, but unlike Job, filial piety involves responsibility, and at times, punitive actions if that responsibility is not exercised. However, the Job paradigm may help bring out some weakness in this kind of African therapy, which will be pointed out later.

49

ENDNOTES

1.   Benjamin Ray, <u>African Religions</u>, (Englewood, New Jersey: Prentice Hall, Inc., 1976), p. 104.

2.   I. Sow, <u>Anthropological Structures of Madness in Black Africa</u>, (New York: International Universities Press, 1980), p. 57-58.

3.   Benjamin Ray, (1976), p. 10.

4.   I. Sow, (1980), p. 57-58.

5.   Ibid.

6.   Ibid., p. 63.

7.   Ibid., p. 78-79.

8.   Ibid.

9.   Ibid.

10.   Ibid.

11.   Ibid.

12.   Ibid.

13.   Ibid.

14.   Ibid., p. 65.

15.   Ibid.

16.   Kofi Appiah-Kubi, <u>Man Cures, God Heals</u>, (New York: Friendship Press, 1981), p. 76.

17.   Ibid.

18.   Eugene L. Mendonsa, <u>Politics of Divination</u>, (Berkeley: University of California, 1982), p. 109.

19.   Ibid.

20.   Ibid., p. 110.

21.   Ibid., p. 113.

22.   Ibid., p. 114.

23.   Vida Francis, "Gaps in Doctor-Patient Communication; Patient's Response to Medical Advice" in <u>Psychosomatic Medicine, Current Journal Articles</u>, compiled by J. Elizabeth Jeffress, (Flushing N.Y.: Medical Examination Pub. Co., 1971), p. 26.

24.   Mendonsa, (1982) p. 117.

50

24. Mendonsa, (1982) p. 117.

25. Victor W. Turner, Ndembu Divination, (London: Manchester University Press, 1961), p. 21.

26. Ibid., p. 8.

27. Ibid., p. 17.

28. I. Sow, (1980) p. 66.

29. Dominique Zahan, The Religion, Spirituality and Thought of Traditional Africans, translated by K. E. Martin and L. M. Martin, (Chicago: University of Chicago Press, 1979), p. 86.

30. Ibid., p. 86.

31. Erwin H. Ackernecht, A Short History of Psychiatry, (New York: Jafner Pub. Co. Inc., 1959), p. 84.

32. Max Gluckman, "Moral Crises: Magical and Secular Solutions" in Max Gluckman (ed) The Allocation of Responsibility, (London: Manchester University Press, 1972), p. 23.

33. Ibid., p. 5.

34. Jack Goody, "Introduction" in Meyer Fortes and Robin Horton (eds) Oedipus and Job in West African Religion, (Cambridge: Cambridge University Press, 1983), p. viii.

35. Ibid., p. ix.

36. Ibid.

37. Meyer Fortes and Robin Horton, Oedipus and Job in West African Religion, p. 13.

38. Ibid., p. 29.

39. Ibid., p. 6.

Chapter 4

An African Therapy in Dialogue with
Freudian Psychoanalysis

Some of the influence of Freud's ideas are already alluded to in the psychological interpretation of the belief or concept of ancestors and their integral role in the kind of African therapy considered. In addition to these indirect influences, Freud's own understanding of the role or influence of ancestors is best represented in his book Totem and Taboo. His attempt in this work was to try to apply his psycho-analytic theory to what he calls "unresolved problems of Social psychology."[1] He attempted to draw close disciplines such as social anthropology, philology, and folklore on the one hand and his psycho-analytic theory on the other.

Freud was interested in this study on the mentality of so-called primitive people such as the Aborigines of Australia. What Freud describes about the belief and function of Totem among the aborigines could be true for the Tallensis of northern Ghana.

Totem is usually an animal, embodying the spirit of ancestor, the founding ancestor of the Clan. The totem symbolizes the guardian spirit of the great ancestor who protects and guides as well as punishes those who do not keep the moral code of the community. Freud, as one might expect, traces the strict observation of moral codes and killing the Totem to an ancestor's historical problem of incest. He posits that in primitive societies,

> I can see nothing against the presumption that it is precisely this incestuous factor in the relation that provides savages with the motive for their rules of avoidance...Thus the explanation which we should adopt for these strictly enforced avoidances among primitive peoples. The same explanation holds good for all other avoidances between both blood and tribal relations.[2]

Totems serve mainly two purposes, the religious and the social.

Religiously they symbolize respect and dependence for protection. Socially, they also symbolize a sense of oneness as member(s) of a clan. Freud suggests that "in the later history of totemism, these two sides, the religious and the social, tend to part company."[3]

This view of Freud is hard to accept based on some knowledge of the so-called primitive that he is

52

discussing. The religious and the social rather reinforced each other. One can hardly exist without the other.

For Freud, the totem animal is the father. The taboos of inhibitions of killing the Totem and not having a sexual encounter with a member of families bound together by a totem "coincide in their content with the two crimes of Oedipus,"[4] who killed his father and married his mother. The child develops both love and hatred towards the father. On killing the father, the child is relieved of hatred but this is replaced by guilt and/or shame. To relieve himself of the conflict of love and guilt towards the father, he displaces "his hostile and fearful feelings on to a substitute,"[5] the totem animal.

Freud's interpretation of the psychological belief or concept of totem seems to be the ambivalent double of love and hate. This was precipitated by what he refers to in his psycho-analysis as "deferred obedience." Freud's conclusion is that "Totemic religion arose from the filial sense of guilt, in an attempt to allay that feeling and to appease the father by deferred obedience to him."[6] As to why these so-called magic acts (divination included) work, Freud offers the following psychological explanation.

First they operate by the "associative theory." People practice it because they have wishes to fulfill, and these wishes are backed by a powerful belief system. So primitive man wishes, believes, and these beliefs are brought to pass because he wills it.[7] They [primitive people] create a satisfying situation by means of centrifugal excitements of the method open to them.[8] According to Freud, these wishes are followed by a mechanical impulse, the will, which is later destined to alter the whole face of the earth in order to satisfy its wishes.[9] "The motor impulse makes a mental picture of the conducive elements that induce satisfaction in such a way that it becomes possible to experience the satisfaction by means of--- motor hallucinations."[10] Later the psychological emphasis on motive shifts to the means by which the act was done. "It does appear as though it is the magical act which owing to its similarity with the desired result alone determines the occurrence of that result."[11]

It is important to appreciate the efforts he made to offer a psychological explanation to those phenomena that are part of many non-western cultures. Some of his explanations may also give insights that may be helpful for therapies within the unique situations of these cultures.

One cannot help but raise a few objections. Freud does acknowledge the deficiencies in his studies. Yet in the application of his theory, Freud seems determined either to explain away whatever he has no answer for or to find a category to fit his theory. It seems, that his theory seeks to explain but cannot be challenged by the data of the research. Freud suggests that magic works because of the mental adjustments in the adherents' minds. In order to justify his thesis, he likens this phenomenon of "magic" to child play. This approach may suggest how unprepared Freud is to accept anything for which he has no answer. He concludes that whatever one wishes and wills and conjures in his mind happens. This seems to be contrary to the sitz im Leb of the so-called primitive people.

The psycho-analytical theory of Freud and its basic anthropological assumptions should be considered. Some further criticisms will be raised out of the anthropological assumptions of Freud. It is important to begin by observing one important aspect in African therapy, the community from which the individual gets his/her identity and strength. The community and the individual members of it are inseparable.

An individual, as a member of a group, family and tribe, is invariably influenced by that group. He/she is influenced by the thoughts, feelings, and characteristics of the group. However, that individual also has some unique qualities that are his/hers. In this regard, Freud suggests that it is easier to determine the differences of that individual from the group than it is "to discover the causes of this difference."[12] What may help to give glimpses of such causes is the phenomena of the unconscious and conscious aspects of a person. For the "unconscious phenomena play an altogether preponderating part not only in organic life, but also in the operation of the intelligence."[13] As compared to the unconscious, the conscious is of little significance. The motivations that drive a person are more the conscious. Referring to the unconscious, Freud further suggests that "...this substratum consists of the innumerable common characteristics handed down from generation to generation, which constitute the genius of a race."[14]

According to Le Bon, as paraphrased by Freud, the learned, unique, individual differences are dissolved into the group identity. "The mental superstructure, the development of which the individual shows such dissimilarities, is removed, and the unconscious foundations, which are similar to everyone stand exposed to view."[15] Hence the individual begins to show common characteristics like those of the Group. But it does not end there. Le Bon suggests that individuals also emerge with new unique characteristics and he gives three reasons for that.

The first reason is that the individual is now able to draw from some instincts that were formerly being restrained. However, Freud rather objects to the idea of new unique qualities emerging. For Freud, what has happened is that "in a group the individual is brought under conditions which allow him to throw off the repressions of his conscious instincts."[16] Freud prefers to look at what he says Le Bon suggests that "the manifestations of this unconscious, in which all that is evil in the human mind is contained as a predisposition."[17]

The second reason is attributed to the contagion principle. Le Bon, as paraphrased by Freud, suggests that individual acts in groups are contagious "and contagious to such a degree that an individual readily sacrifices his personal interest to the collective interest."[18]

The third reason is based on the principle of suggestibility. It is a process by which an individual loses his/her conscious personality. The individual, by living and interacting with members of the group, be it family, race, or nationality, acquires the suggestions sent out by the group. This principle is best illustrated by hypnotism, when the conscious personality is lost to the hypnotist and controlled by him/her. In summary, the individual loses conscious personality to the group. He/She is immersed in the unconscious, and by means of contagion and suggestion, the principal characteristics of the group are acquired by the individual.[19]

This theory does offer very important insights into the dynamics of community life in Africa, especially life in groups such as the family, clan, or even tribe in Africa. However, it has problems. It appears to make the individual 'robot-like' with no will, annihilating the conscious personality. It may be repressed but can hardly be dissolved altogether. Furthermore, as suggested by Freud, "...the contagion seems actually to be a manifestation of the suggestibility."[20] So the separation between them seems arbitrary.

The individuality of this person seems trapped by the group. Hence individuals may not make a difference. This image of the individual within a group or community does seem not to correspond wholly to the notion of individual and the clan, the tribe, or nation. For there are many instances in history of individuals who rose above the community, and challenged the communities. These are the makers of History, with a Capital H. They are the heroes. If individuals in groups were so trapped that they lost their unique individuality, there would be no place for the changes these heroes effect.

This may further be supported by a proverb among the Tallensis of Northern Ghana that "ba duot bii ka bu dot ka yin ne" translated roughly (they give birth to a child, but they do not determine the future of that child).

The individual personality at times may be selfish, but that personality is checked by the collective identity of the community. In some cases the cruel and destructive powers of the instincts of the group are challenged by the individual powers of perception. The double of love and hatred mentioned earlier is both necessary and helpful here to bring harmony and progress to both the group as a unit and the individuals within the unit.

Though Freud objects to this theory, as I do, with the conclusions of Le Bon and others such as McDougall, he feels the notion of suggestibility is actually an "irreducible, primitive phenomenon, a fundamental fact in the mental life of man."[21] Suggestibility works because it uses emotions as an ally. These emotions are the manifestations of instinctive activities. Freud uses his notion of libido or love to explain why emotions can induce individual group psychology. The libido or love felt by an individual especially aims at an expression of union with the other that he/she is directed to. However, that is only possible in sex. In other situations, the same tendency (need for union) is not to that same extent. Nevertheless, the instincts maintain the original intention -- union. The group then may be held together by this power of Eros or Libido. The individual does give up his/her destructiveness to the group and allows the group to influence him/her by suggestion. "He does it because he feels the need of being in harmony with them rather than in opposition to them -- so that perhaps after all he does it "ihnen zu Lieb" (for love of them). These psychological and psychoanalytic interpretations of the essence of the community and the individual do offer some insights that could inform and give some directions as to the kind of African therapy that can be pursued. Most African therapy inevitably involves the community. There is no doubt that these analyses have many deficiencies in them; nevertheless, they are attempts to look at African beliefs and concepts from without.

What will follow is an examination of Freud's psychoanalysis and its anthropological assumptions.

The psyche, according to Freud, can be divided into two parts: namely, the brain from where human actions come and the human actions themselves which are important data. The gap between the brain and the conscious actions is a region of unknown.[22] The oldest agent of the psyche is the Id. It has inherited qualities, much of which is still unknown by modern science.

From the influence of the external world, the psyche has another specialized portion. This is referred to as Ego. The Ego's chief function is self-preservation. It receives all the influences of the external world. It processes the data from the external world in such a way that it can respond to the outside to its own advantage of self-preservation.[23]

The Id is responsible to the internal world. Its main task is to control the instincts by deciding what is appropriate to express, when and how. The Id is guided by the rule of pleasure. Hence it decides when and how to derive maximum pleasure.

During childhood, the child depends on parents. The feeling of dependence becomes a depot for the (data for the Ego), a "special agency in which this parental influence is prolonged. This is called super-ego."[24] The Super-Ego is different from the Ego and at times opposes it. The Super-Ego becomes a third force with which the Ego must reckon.

An act can mostly be successfully executed if it meets the demands of the Id, the Ego and the Super-Ego. The correlation between relationship and function of the Ego and the Super-Ego according to Freud is influenced by the personalities of parents and their "family, racial and national traditions handed on through them, as well as the demands of the immediate social milieu which they represent."[25]

However, the Super-Ego does have influences from others of significance such as teachers, pastors, etc. The common bond between the Ego and the Super-Ego is that "they both represent the influences of the past."26

The influences of the Id are hereditary. The Ego also represents the growing experience of the individual. According to Freud, instincts are those forces which strive to satisfy the needs of the Id at whatever cost. He suggests that instincts can be reduced to two basic types: the Eros and the destructive instincts. Eros tries to preserve itself and other species, i.e., self-love and love of other objects. The aim of Eros "is to establish ever greater unities and to preserve them thus...to bind together."27 The aim of destructive instinct is "to undo connections and so to destroy things."28 It is referred to as the death instinct.

Summary of Personality in Freud's Psychoanalysis

Psychoanalysis was originally a part of the medical sciences. However, it slowly gained acceptance in the human sciences. Its method is basically clinical, derived from empirical observation of the human species.

Psychoanalysis makes certain anthropological assumptions. These include the following: Every human action can be accounted for (Freud calls this the "psychic determinism"). Human actions derive their energies from libido. Through therapy, "the forces of the unconscious can be brought under control. (Freedom is knowledge; slavery is ignorance.)"29

Personality in Freudian psychoanalysis has three dimensions, physiological, social, and psychological. Personality in the physiological dimension is comprised of biological make-ups of organisms. These are what Freud calls "instincts, drives, instinctual drives, sexuality, psychosexuality or libido."30 This physiological dimension is more dominant in childhood when the Ego is unable to assert controls. Personality in Freudian psychoanalysis is made of dichotomy. The struggle between drive and controls, need for expression against repression, Eros against death, narcissism against autism, cathexes and counter cathexes, and Ego against Id.

The social dimension is an important and inevitable one. Everyone is born into a society with

58

some established traditions or ways of life. These traditions, or customs, give rise to "an inevitable conflict between the instinct-ridden and poorly controlled child and the adults responsible for approved behaviours."[31]

Psychologically, the interplay between the Id, Ego, and Super-Ego results in some conflicts early in a child's life. These may result in some degree of psychological sickness "because of frustrating early experiences which then become crystallized in certain inner states."[32]

As helpful as Freud's psychoanalytical constructions may be, the author has a few objections to them. Freud made up some brain myths to justify his abstract speculative description of psychological phenomena with hypothetical brain structures.

Although he believed he was following the scientific empirical method, one has difficulties finding the empirical data upon which he drew his conclusion. Obviously he drew his conclusion from observation but it is hard to present absolute truths from observation. For observations are subjective as they are colored by different influences, some of which he himself recognized.

Freud may have been greatly influenced by Charles Darwin. Darwin is said to have "proposed a psychology based on instincts (e.g., sex and aggression) and thought of development in genetic terms."[33] These ideas of instincts and genetic development seemed to be adapted by Freud in his psychoanalysis. Freud seems to follow Darwin's theory in developing his theory that primitive man was wicked and despotic, but he has not provided any evidence. Even the animals which informed Darwin in his theory, do not live brutal and despotic lives with their young ones. If anything, they teach the essence of what the word Care is all about. As further observed by Hogan, "most anthropologists would rather argue that a tribe whose adult males were not joined together as a cohesive social unit would have been at a serious competitive disadvantage in the struggle to survive."[34]

For Freud, the unconscious is very important in his psychoanalysis. Unfortunately Freud does not provide a definite definition of the unconscious. It seems he used it in about three different ways. In one sense, he used it to refer to mental elements repressed. There is no direct voluntary contact between them and the mind.

Freud also used it to refer to the available data that was never imparted to the individual by parent, family, or society through experience.

Finally, he used it to refer to those acts that happen in childhood before the child can express in words what those acts were.

Freud, it seems, uses instincts arbitrarily as units between psychoanalysis and biology. One could admit that an excess of primary process thinking can be pathological but primary process thinking could include fantasies, egocentric and perhaps hallucinatory.[35] Later, Freud seems to doubt his own psychological physiology of instincts. He admits that the notion of instincts may only be mythological. Hence, he admits the possibility of not seeing them.[36]

According to Freud, the acting out of the sexual instincts seems to harm the normal course of civilized or societal life, so society exerts control over it. However, if the controls are just depriving the individual of pleasure, the individual feels unhappy. The longer society holds the controls, the higher the chances of the individual becoming neurotic, but if society allows free expression of the instinct, "the vicissitudes of the instincts would make free and uninhibited gratification impossible."[37] Therefore, either way of handling the instinct has destructive consequences to the individual. The instinct seems to lead to more misery than joy. Rief expresses this dilemma aptly when he observes that "Freud...comes to the tacit understanding that sex really is nasty, an ignoble slavery to nature."[38]

With these objections in mind, a summary of the process of psychotherapy based on Freudian psychoanalytical theory as outlined by Fine will be presented here. This will help focus on the similarities and differences between it and African therapy as outlined in the earlier pages.

The time of treatment ranges between one to five hours. It starts with a face-to-face encounter with the therapist. After that, the patient shifts to the couch. The session on the couch is between forty-five minutes and one hour.

The patient is asked to say whatever comes to his/her mind. This is known as free association, the first fundamental rule. While on the couch, the patient's main task is to talk and express feelings, memories, and associations.

The analyst disappears to somewhere, generally behind the patient. The analyst makes comments, may reflect something to the patient, asks questions for clarification, or just hears what is being said. The treatment could last between one and ten years. The analyst generally has some idea(s) of the direction, goals. "The main stages of the process for most analysts are establishing a relationship, having an analytic honeymoon, experiencing a first treatment crisis, deepening of the therapy, working through termination."39

At a follow up session, the patient comes for treatment at a set time and pays a set price. The patient continues to speak about whatever comes to mind. In addition to talking, the patient must observe his/her body movements and note them on paper. They are given to the analyst. The point of this process is to help the patient develop some awareness of himself/herself.

The analyst's task is to listen, support, and try to bring to the conscious level what the client may have been unconscious of. The particular emphasis is on those issues about which the patient has a great deal of difficulty expressing his/her feelings or acting on. There should be little or no attempt to offer advice, give suggestions, or even affirm any direct intervention in the patient's life.40

Mechanisms of the Therapy

On the patient's part, he/she is expected to increase his/her sense of awareness of how he/she functions as a person. The analyst on the other hand, is to focus on dealing with resistances and transferences. The patient should understand the resistances as part of reality from a psychological make-up and not reality in itself.41

Resistance, according to Fine, can be divided into two. The first is direct resistance which occurs when the patient is not being punctual, not paying fees on time, not talking, and when talking, lying. The second is indirect resistance which consists of

> overemphasis on reality; unreasonable demands; negative therapeutic reactions, in which the patient gets worse in spite of being able to verbalize all interpretations; transference excesses; somatization; acting out; excessive regression; excessive emotionality; and absence of feeling.42

The therapist on his/her part must accept the patient with openness, and the patient's free associations. "The patient acquires a series of insights. These insights represent the core of analytic growth process."[43]

Transference and countertransference also play an important part in the whole process. Transference helps to focus on the way the patient resists. Perhaps, the therapist represents something or somebody assuming a reality to the patient. However, the analyst has an obligation to work on his/her countertransference to disprove the patient's transference. For Fine, "the working through of the transferences and resistances are of inestimable value to the patient in clarifying conflicts with people on the outside. These conflicts are also the result of the unconscious transferences."[44]

The patient is helped to come to terms with the fact that "his view of reality is distorted by his emotional preconceptions. As his emotional reactions become resolved he begins to see reality more and more clearly."[45] While being able to intellectualize is important, it must be balanced with the patient's ability to feel. But feelings should also be clarified. As the patient comes to terms with feelings, the defense mechanisms devised by the patient will give way.[46] Other factors important to psychoanalysis are the simplicity of the language used, and the extent to which the analyst himself/herself has undergone psychoanalysis.

Summary of African Therapy

In order to be able to point out the differences between African therapy and Freudian psychoanalysis, the former will be sketched here.

In African therapy, the patient is not usually encouraged to gain insights to achieve independence from others. Rather, the therapy seeks to involve the patient as a direct offender or a victim of an offense. Some ritual acts help to remove the act (offense) that contaminated the social order. The patient, in some cases, is considered a social victim in order to address the wrong and not as direct punishment for any offense he/she personally has committed. Cures are arrived at by performing the appropriate ritual as well as integrating the patient into the community. In some cases, cure is said to be effected if the broken social order is reconstituted. African therapy seeks to grasp some meaning out of the sickness or misfortune.

It is the task of the African therapist to put the cause of sickness into an appropriate social-cultural context. He/she does this through symbolical configurations which may help to relate the offense to a past life and its consequences for the present, with implication for the future. This attempt may not have any direct bearing on any childhood trauma and does not necessarily trace its root to the intrapsychical past history of the patient. Indeed, in some cases, it does not even reflect the past behavior of the patient involved. What may be at stake in this kind of therapy is the past, both collective and individual, which has moral implication for both collective and individual consequences.

The basic message for healing in African therapy can be summarized thus. Your sickness, misfortune, or condition can be traced to either an inappropriate action by one member of the family or a conflict that existed among members of the family who may now be dead. The purpose of the therapy is to say to the offender, (*You have done wrong or wrong was done by someone else, we have accepted responsibility, confessed the guilt/shame/damage by an appropriate ritual.*) If it was a past conflict, descendants of the parties who gave rise to the conflict do the confession on behalf of the dead.[47] The effect of this kind of African therapy could be its power to integrate the offender and offense into the community without outright condemnation, guilt-induced mechanisms, or any form of brutality or vengeance. This could increase the person's (either victim of or direct offender) sense of belonging and invoke the capacity to accept, to love, himself/herself and others within the community. Freedom with responsibility is restored to the patient.

These virtues are indispensable in most African communities.[48] As correctly pointed out by Mendonsa, "the symbols of the divinary process are repositories of the information about the major structural values of culture."[49] These symbols help to provide meaning by offering a symbolic language to communicate to patient and community at complex levels, "values associated with deeply meaningful ancestral codes."[50]

Similarities

From the briefs of Freudian psychoanalysis and African therapy, one cannot help but note the similarities as well as differences. First the similarities.

In both, there is either someone who comes personally for help or one coming to seek help on behalf of someone else.

In both, there is a therapist whose primary function is similar -- to listen, reflect, interpret, and help provide a sense of direction. In both, the ability and personality of the therapist are important elements.

In both, the therapist is a neutral person. The therapist should not be a blood relative.

In both, there is a code of communication or guide of communication.

The Differences

While the emphasis of African therapy is mostly on the interpersonal, Freudian psychoanalysis seems to emphasize intrapsychical. However, both do not have to be either exclusively interpersonal or intrapsychical.

In African therapy, the social web of the patient is very important, perhaps indispensable, whereas in Freudian psychoanalysis it may be possible to complete the therapy without directly calling on the community or involving the community.

In African therapy, symbols play an important role as the language of communication. In psychoanalysis the symbols are avoided as much as possible because the language should be verbal and as simple as possible.

An African therapy cannot be complete without some form of ritual, such as drinking, eating, or sacrifice. In psychoanalysis, that is not mentioned or given attention.

Whereas divination as a kind of African therapy traces its roots to the religio-magical tradition of healing, the Freudian psychoanalysis seems to have its roots in naturalistic or scientific traditions of healing.

In African therapy, religion enhances, or is supposed to enhance or is considered an integral part of healing. In psychoanalysis, religion may be suspected as an ally to the cause of the problem and attempts may be made to free the victim from religion.

In spite of these differences, the author believes these two kinds of therapies can still work together. At least they can play complimentary roles to each other. Some Africans such as Masamba ma

64

Mpolo, Emmanuel Yartekwei Lartey, Ibrahim Sow, to name a few, have attempted this. The author is writing from an African perspective. For that reason, the emphasis will be on how the Freudian psychoanalysis may play a complimentary role to African therapy, especially in pastoral counseling.

ENDNOTES

1.   Sigmund Freud, Totem and Taboo, (New York: Norton, 1952), p. ix.

2.   Ibid., p. 16.

3.   Ibid., p. 104.

4.   Ibid., p. 132.

5.   Ibid., p. 129.

6.   Ibid., p. 145.

7.   Ibid., p. 83.

8.   Ibid., p. 84.

9.   Ibid.

10.   Ibid.

11.   Ibid.

12.   Sigmund Freud, Group Psychology and the Analysis of Ego, Authorized translation by James Strachey, (New York: Liveright Pub. Co. 1951), p. 7.

13.   Ibid., p. 8.

14.   Ibid.

15.   Ibid., p. 9.

16.   Ibid., p. 9-10.

17.   Ibid., p. 10.

18.   Ibid., p. 11.

19.   Ibid.

20.   Ibid., p. 13.

21.   Ibid., p. 35.

22.   Sigmund Freud, An Outline of Psycho-Analysis, translated by James Strachey, (New York: W. W. Norton and Co., 1949), p. 1.

23.   Ibid., p. 2.

24.   Ibid., p. 3.

25.   Ibid.

26.   Ibid., p. 4.

27.   Ibid., p. 5.

28.   Ibid.

29.   Reuben Fine, "Psychoanalysis" in Raymond Corsini's (ed) Current Psychotherapies, (Itasca: F. E. Peacock Pub. Inc., 1973), p. 7.

30.   Ibid., p. 10.

31.   Ibid., p. 11.

32.   Ibid.

33.   Robert Hogan, Personality Theory: The Personological Tradition, (Englewood, N.J.: Prentice Hall, Inc., 1976), p. 22.

34.   Ibid., p. 47.

35.   Ibid., p. 27.

36.   Sigmund Freud, Introductory Lectures on Psychoanalysis, translated by James Strachey, (New York: W. W. Norton Co., 1966), p. 95.

37.   Robert Hogan, p. 37.

38.   P. Rief, Freud: The Mind of the Moralist, (New York: Doubleday, 1959), p. 170.

39.   Reuben Fine in Raymond Corsini, 1973, p. 20.

40.   Ibid.

41.   Ibid.

42.   Ibid., p. 20.

43.   Ibid.

44.   Ibid., p. 21.

45.   Ibid.

46.   Ibid.

47.   Eugene Mendonsa, The Politics of Divination, 1982.

48.   Ibid.

49.   Ibid., p. 141.

50.   Ibid.

Chapter 5

African Therapy in Dialogue with
Persuasion Healing Approach

The Persuasion and Healing thesis of Frank is an attempt to find a common ground for all forms of therapies, both western and non-western. Frank believes that in spite of the many differences in the various schools of therapy there are some basic guides that can be traced in all forms of therapies. These basic guides or ingredients make therapies work. The basic guides also make them adaptable to different situations by different people.

He believes each therapy has some validity in its own way of achieving results. An attempt is made here to briefly present Frank's view, and compare it to African therapy.

Frank is of the view that every person is made up of the influences of the family (whether in the Western immediate family or African extended family) and the society. Every person's value systems are derived from these sources. Therefore, treatment for Frank may be effective when a person's well-being is secured, that is, if these value systems operate coherently and consistently.

In every society, those who perform the functions that help value systems operate coherently and consistently are called healers. The ways one goes about ensuring the well-being of others in a society are many and varied. The performing act and art of inducing or securing the well-being of individuals is what Frank refers to as psychotherapy.[1]

In his understanding, in psychotherapy there is one person who is so-designated healer and another who is designated sufferer or patient. There is usually a set of circumstances in which the healer seeks to induce well-being in an individual who is said to be suffering. An important element here is some form of belief that healing could be effected by such means as words, acts, and rituals in which healer, patient, and community participate together.[2] Based on this understanding, Frank suggests that "the administration of an inert medicine by a doctor to a patient is also analogous to psychotherapy. Its effectiveness depends on its symbolization of the physician's healing function, which produces favorable changes in the patient's feelings and attitudes."[3] In his view, psychotherapy works partly because of the "shared belief of participants." This for him is the reason for the different methods "in different societies and historical epochs"[4] in different societies.

Modern psychotherapy may be traced to two traditions of healing historically: 1) the religio-magical and 2) the naturalistic or scientific.

The religio-magical tradition which is as old as humanity, considers ill health as caused supernaturally. The scientific does not. The relationship between these two traditions is discussed in detail in my first volume.[5]

Frank does offer an instructive insight worth noting.

> Psychotherapies in societies or groups with a primarily religious world view are based on religio-magical theories...healing rituals...with religious rites. The scientific world view of western societies is reflected in a tendency to regard psychotherapy as a form of medical treatment, based on scientific understanding of human nature.[6]

What may seem to be generally true may be that every form of treatment reflects to some degree the societal values. Even within a given society, people in a particular social and/or economic group may be more inclined to prefer one form of treatment to another. For instance, Frank suggests that in America, people in a lower economic class may prefer "directive treatment whereas, middle and upper-class patients, who put a high value on self-knowledge and self-direction, are more likely to receive permissive forms of treatment stressing insight."[7]

In normal everyday living, one comes across situations that destablize one's equanimity. The individual's inability to deal with crisis results in a stress. The stress could be short-lived or long-lived. Hence Frank suggests that psychotherapy "...can...be a temporary or persistent unsuccessful adaptation to stress."[8] According to Frank, there may be two types of people who suffer from maladaptive mechanisms and seek help in psychotherapy: 1) Those who are physically disabled by diseases or genetically traced problems, and 2) those whose maladaptive mechanisms resulted from interpersonal experience.

Frank offers the following explanations for the causes of stresses and, in some cases, maladaptive mechanisms. To live and function in the world, every person has to form an "assumed world." The assumed world of an individual is a system of

> a highly structured, complex interacting set of values, expectations, and images of oneself and others, which guide and in turn are guided by a person's perceptions and behavior and which are closely related to his [her] emotional states and -- feelings of well-being.9

Some assumptions change more rapidly than others. Some assumptions are also more lasting while others are temporary.

A small portion of the "assumed world" may be conscious. However, what may be conscious at a given time may not be conscious at another time.

The assumed world may also differ in its scale of common agreement and conflict. Frank suggests that the internal conflicts are responsible for conflicts' distresses.10

Frank also divides the "assumptive worlds" into two, the healthy and the unhealthy assumptive systems respectively. According to him, the

> Healthy assumptive systems are characterized by internal consistency and close correspondence with actual conditions. They thus lead to reliable, satisfactory interactions with other persons, accompanied by a sense of competence, inner security, and well-being, which enables them to be readily modified when necessary.11

The unhealthy assumptive systems on the other hand are

> internally full of conflict and do not accurately correspond to circumstances, leading to experiences of frustration and failure. Efforts to cope with or evade these feelings tend to intensify distortions and conflicts and to become both self-perpetuating and self-defeating, resulting in cumulative adaptional difficulties.12

For Frank, the purpose of psychotherapy is to attempt to provide the person with relief from distress; correct errors, which improves functioning; and subsequently "resolve conflicts in his assumptions concerning himself [herself] and others."13

Frank's treatment of illness in primitive societies echoes some of the views of the author in his first volume, referred to earlier. The basic beliefs about illness among many primary societies include the following. Illness may be individual but has corporate implications. Illness may be caused by disobedience to the moral code of the community. Illness may also be inflicted by external agents such as spirits, hence the healing process includes both the individual and the society. Furthermore, the place of rituals and healers in the assumptive system of the society are necessary factors to their effectiveness in healing. Both ritual and healer reinforce each other.

In the ritual the patient's sense of worth may be reinforced. The support of his/her ethnic group may show acceptance. The active role of the patient may help bring the patient out of his/her self-absorption and also induce a sense of participation.

There may, in some cases, be confessions implicitly or explicitly. The confessional element in healing may have some potential to relieve guilt and/or shame and experience acceptance of self and by community. Frank's emphasis is that these forms of healing work because they form part of the assumption of patient in his/her society. The healing methods

> involve an interplay between patient, healer, group, and the world of supernatural, which serves to raise the patient's expectancy of cure, help him to harmonize his inner conflicts, integrate him with his group and the spirit world, supply a conceptual frame work to aid this, and stir him emotionally. In the process they combat his anxiety and strengthen his sense of self-worth.[14]

As to why primitive healing may be effective, Frank thinks the success of healers in primary cultures may be attributed to the faith of the patients. He comes to this conclusion from clinical experiments, especially one with three particular patients. The first patient had a chronic inflammation of the gall bladder with stones. The second could not recover from a major abdominal surgery and the third was almost dying of cancer.

A highly respected faith healer was told to treat these patients from a distance without the patients' knowledge. He observed that it did not change their situations.

The second time, he told the patients about this faith healer and did everthing he could to raise their expectations and told the patients that the faith healer would start treating them. But he told the faith healer not to treat them and made sure he complied. The three patients improved. The second became completely cured. The other two showed some response for a time. The cancer patient who was anemic recovered and went home. The gall bladder patient also partially recovered, went home and did not have a recurrence for some years.[15]

Frank further correlates the success of faith healers or healers in primary societies to the notion of placebo in pharmacology. Placebo refers to an inert substance the doctor may give to the patient to relieve distress in replacement of a sedative or addictive drug. Placebo, Frank suggests, may effect healing because of its symbolic power.16 The symbolic power of placebo may be derived from the symbolic power of a doctor who prescribes it.17 The role of the doctor in the community evokes "expectancy trust" in the patient. It may be this "expectancy trust" that effects the healing. This may raise the question of deception on the part of the doctor and placebo. The question of deception may have limited the use of placebo or at least made doctors conscious of the role of placebo in the doctor-patient relations. However, placebo does play a role in effecting some types of treatment on some types of patients, especially in psychosomatic illness and treatment and in some psychiatric cases.

Frank attempts to apply the placebo factor in medicine to psychotherapy. He writes, "If part of the success of all forms of psychotherapy may be attributed to the therapist's ability to mobilize the patient's expectation of help, then some of the effects of psychotherapy should be similar to those produced by a placebo."18 As a working hypothesis, he suggests "part of the healing power of all forms of psychotherapy lives in their ability to mobilize the patients' hopes of relief."19

One important principle of Frank's thesis is the principle of persuasion in everyday encounter with implications for psychotherapy.

Frank has delved into a great deal of research data to prove his thesis. In the healer-patient encounter, participation on the part of the healer increases the patient's susceptibility.20 This is even true if the patient is to undertake an initiative. Research has shown that "the content of a person's speech can be influenced by faint clues of approval or disapproval given by his listener, and that the amount of this influence is independent of how aware he is of it."21

The implication of this research for therapy, according to Frank, is that "even the most 'nondirective' therapist may influence the patient's speech in the direction of his own wishes, without the awareness of either."22

Summary of Frank's Psychotherapy

For Frank, psychotherapy may be divided into two parts, a) the relationship between the therapist and the patient and b) the therapeutic session.

A) The Therapist and the Patient

According to Frank, although there are a number of schools of psychotherapy, there are also some basic common patterns found in most, if not all, forms of psychotherapy.[23]

1) The encounter is more determined by the therapist than the patient. However, the patient does have some influence on how his/her concerns are made known to the therapist in order for the therapist to understand him/her.

2) A certain level of trust of the therapist by the patient is necessary. The therapist must be perceived by the patient as capable of helping. This calls for an attitude of the therapist that will enhance the "expectancy trust." The therapist has to show an attitude of honesty, sincerity, acceptance, and counter trust on the patient's ability to work through his/her problem.

This atmosphere or quality of the relationship is necessary if the patient is to achieve his/her objective in psychotherapy.

B) The Therapeutic Encounter

Some of the components of psychotherapeutic encounter include emotional, cognitive, and behavioral.[24] In psychotherapy, the emotional level and the "qualitative emotional experience" are very important. Psychotherapy helps the emotional life of an individual "to combat disintegrating emotions that hamper the patient's ability to profit from new experiences and to foster those that facilitate experimentation and personality integration."[25] Psychotherapy could be said to be effective if it "helps the patient to substitute hope for despair, courage for fear, self-confidence for feelings of inferiority."[26]

An element in the therapy which may enhance healing is novelty. Novelty increases hope and induces positive or healthy emotional responses.[27]

Frank further suggests that "cognitively, psychotherapeutic methods supply the patient with new

74

information about himself or...new way of conceptualizing what he already knows."28 This will enable the patient to adjust his assumptive world.

Accordng to Frank, psychotherapy is to be effective of both emotional and cognitive awareness if it results in changes in behavior. However, there is a dynamic relationship among the emotional, cognitive, and behavioral.

Frank classifies therapeutic methods into two categories. These are the directive and the evocative. Directive therapies "try directly to bring about changes in the patient's behavior which, it is believed, will overcome his symptoms or resolve the problems for which he sought treatment."29 This may be done through advice, persuasion, or with some technique like relaxation exercise. Evocative therapies on the other hand

> try to create a situation that will evoke the full gamut of the patient's difficulties and capabilities, thereby enabling him not only to work out better solutions for the problems bringing him to treatment but also to gain greater maturity, spontaneity and inner freedom, so that he becomes better equipped to deal with future stresses as well as current ones.30

Both therapist and patient are concerned with understanding the nature of the problems of the patient. However, while directive emphasizes the understanding of the problems by the patient, evocative therapy emphasizes the patient's understanding of all of his/her life as a whole.31

Directive therapies usually deal mostly with how the patient adjusts to present problems, to enable the therapist to understand how the patient arrived at the present problem. They may not pay much attention to the feelings of the patient in the therapeutic process.

Evocative therapies cover more ground. They deal with present problems, the past, dreams, and fantasies. The feelings of the patient towards the therapist are of interest in evocative therapies.

Evaluation of Persuasion and Healing

Frank attempts to find a common basis of psychotherapy, whether in American or in primary societies and in both religious and secular realms. In many ways, he has made some contributions to therapy in general and African therapy in particular.

In spite of some of the insightful thoughts in his thesis, there are some areas of concern that may be worth pointing out.

Frank attempts a comparative study of psychotherapy with no indication of the potential or real differences and similarities in the various schools of psychotherapy.

Furthermore, he does not attempt to at least mention, let alone to deal with in detail, any psychological theory or theories in the various schools of psychotherapy. The words of Kubie in his review are shared here. He says that after a careful reading of the book, he feels that "there are grains of truth in almost every word that is written, but that these are buried in gritty sands of unspoken and prior assumptions."32

In response to what may be Frank's exaggerated forms of common methods, Kubie observes that in order to know better the "intrinsic nature of any one of the psychotherapies, ...each must be studied objectively and in microscopic detail as a process, before any comparative evaluations are made."33 Kubie does not agree with Frank's basic assumption that the purpose of all psychotherapy may be "an attempt to heal by persuasion." For Kubie, "persuasion is more often than not a psycho-noxious contamination of the therapeutic process."34 According to Kubie, therapists resort to persuasion when therapists may be sensing failure. It is "an impatient effort to find shortcut to a simulation of health."35 Kubie admits that persuasion may be used in palliative therapy but rejects the idea of Frank that it is a core of psychotherapy. Kubie does agree with what Frank may be implying that "psychotherapy can never alter the etiologic processes which produce psychopathology."36 One other failure of Frank, according to Kubie, is a failure "to clarify the intimate interplay between psycho-noxious and psychotherapeutic influences in the course of every form of psychotherapy, whether placebo or psychological, whether religious revivialism or thought-reform, analytic or non-analytic."37 On placebo effects, Kubie's only objection is that it has been used to generalize rather than particularize.

There are also some important words used by Frank which are not defined. These include "assumptives systems," and "healthy and unhealthy images."

Abroms like Kubie agrees that persuasion is not the sole primary cause for therapeutic change in a

76

patient. But Abroms is of the view that persuasion plays an important role in promoting therapeutic change.

Perhaps a case can be made for persuasion by extension of the communication theory advanced by Haley. According to Haley, "...a basic communication theory demonstrates that it is impossible for a person to avoid defining or taking control of definition of his relationship with another."38

This rule provides that "...all messages are not only reports but they also influence or command.... Even if one tries not to influence another person by remaining silent, his silences become an influencing factor in the interchange."39 By application of this theory, a therapist does influence a patient in one way or other. It may be practically impossible to have a neutral therapist in a neutral therapeutic encounter.

According to Abroms, the therapeutic process could be looked at from a transactionalist view. If so conceived, "...the exchange of persuasive messages is all that happens in therapy."40

In this regard, Abroms is of the view that Haley "would contend that the analyst's [including Kubie] purpose of clarifying and revealing his patient's unconscious strivings often masks the very different, underlying aim of persuading the patient to behave in a manner acceptable to the analyst."41

Abroms cites Freud as admitting suggestion as an element in his psychoanalysis. Freud is quoted to have said, "...we readily admit that the results of psychoanalysis rest upon a basis of suggestion...influence on a person through and by means of the transference manifestations of which he is capable."42

Abroms compares persuasion in therapy to a skin graft; it is not all skin grafts that survive. Survival does not always depend on the skillfulness of the surgeon. There are important conditions that make skin grafts survive. These are:

> 1) the grafted tissues must be antigenitically related to the host's own tissue. 2) The old tissue must accept the new as 'self' and not 'other.' 3) The host tissue must supply the new tissue with blood vessels and metabolities and must constantly replace its worn out cells.43

For Abroms then, "Psychotherapeutic change is due to persuasion only in the sense that a graft take is due to surgery. The rest of the process involves the patient's active incorporation."44

The point Abroms is making here is that the analogy attempts to explain "...the process of behavioral incorporation, the mutual role of interpersonal transactions and the intrapsychic event."[45]

In other words, Abroms may be alluding to the fact that persuasion may be effective, indeed may touch the psychic not because it came from a therapist, but because both the interpersonal and intrapsychical dimension of the patient can incorporate the issues raised in the therapy.

He does broaden the argument by including the psychic life of a personality which Frank did not clearly deal with and which may have made some analysts like Kubie disagree vehemently with him.

The Differences and Similarities between Persuasion and Healing and African Therapy

Unlike some other psychotherapies or psychotherapeutic methods, Frank's method has been partly influenced by his African experience. Indeed, he devotes some pages to an African kind of therapy he encountered. Nevertheless, there are a few differences and similarities.

Differences

1.   While African therapy may be based on psychoreligious and anthropological assumptions, the persuasion and healing method does not have any such definite assumptions.

2.   There are different aspects in an African healing process that make healing possible, but persuasion and healing see healing possible simply because of the power of persuasion of the healer.

3.   In African therapy catharsis may have an important place but not in the persuasion and healing thesis.

4.   One important element of African therapy is the use of symbols but persuasion and healing as a method does not mention symbols.

Similarities

1.   In discussing his method with reference to an African context, Frank accepts the various aspects and processes of healing into his method.

2.   Both agree that the social-cultural perceptions of the role of healer are imperative to his powers to effect healing.

3.   Both do agree that there is an element of training necessary.

In spite of these differences and similarities, the Persuasion and Healing method seems to have conceptualized an aspect of African therapy. Persuasion and healing may have helped Africans to label some of their methods of healing as persuasion. The faith of the patient in the healer has been prominently given recognition. Hitherto, these have always been implied but not categorically labeled as therapeutic principles. One African psychiatrist who has attempted to apply Frank's methods more elaborately and consciously from Africa is Kiev.[46]

It is hoped that other Africans will take these concepts and the criticisms of them and develop more systematic and psychological methods of psychotherapy in Africa.

ENDNOTES

1.   Jerome D. Frank, <u>Persuasion and Healing</u>, (New York: Schocken Books, 1964), p. 1.

2.   Ibid., p. 3.

3.   Ibid.

4.   Ibid.

5.   Abraham A. Berinyuu, <u>Pastoral Care to Sick in Africa</u>, (Frankfurt: Peter Lang, 1988).

6.   Frank, p. 7.

7.   Ibid.

8.   Ibid., p. 19.

9.   Ibid., p. 21.

10.   Ibid., p. 25.

11.   Ibid., p. 35.

12.   Ibid.

13.   Ibid.

14.   Ibid., p. 53.

15.   Ibid., p. 61.

16.   Ibid., p. 66.

17.   Ibid.

18.   Ibid., p. 71.

19.   Ibid., p. 72.

20.   Ibid., p. 112.

21.   Ibid., p. 113.

22.   Ibid.

23.   Ibid., p. 115.

24.   Ibid., p. 143.

25.   Ibid., p. 144.

26.   Ibid.

27.   Ibid.

28.   Ibid., p. 145.

29.   Ibid., p. 148.

30.   Ibid.

31.   Ibid.

32.   L. S. Kubie, "Review of Persuasion and Healing" in <u>Journal of Nervous and Mental Diseases</u>, vol. 133, 1961, p. 561.

33.   Ibid., p. 562.

34.   Ibid., p. 563.

35.   Ibid., p. 564.

36.   Ibid., p. 563.

37.   Jay Haley, <u>Strategies of Psychotherapy</u>, (New York: Grune and Stratton, 1963), p. 9-10.

38.   Ibid.

39.   Ibid.

40.   Gene M. Abroms, "Persuasion In Psychotherapy" in <u>The American Journal of Psychiatry</u>, vol. 124, No. 9, March, 1968, p. 12-18.

41.   Ibid.

42.   Ibid.

43.   Ibid.

44.   Ibid.

45.   Ibid.

46.   Ari Kiev, <u>Magic, Faith and Healing</u>, (New York: The Fortress, 1964).

Chapter 6

Helpful Hints for African Therapy

In the previous two chapters, an African therapy and its dialogue with Freudian psychoanalysis were discussed. The similarities and differences were noted. An attempt will be made now to see how Freudian psychoanalysis could be complimentary to the kind of African therapy being considered.

The kind of African therapy being discussed seems to be predominantly a community affair. It also seems to emphasize more behavioral than developmental. In other words, therapy seems to solicit appropriate behavior in a given situation, at a given time, to a given person. It does not seem to offer any explanation for behaviors that may trace their causes to developmental circumstances.

Even though African therapy does achieve its desired results, it could do more if it also dealt with the developmental as well. For the fact is that there are developmental problems in Africa as in other continents. There are some aspects of African life that may show that the developmental reasons in therapy may be necessary. These include the role of authority figures such as fathers, mothers, chiefs, and ancestors, to name a few. In some patriarchal societies, the father usually has all rights of discipline. In a home of this kind of father, his authority may be absolute. No member of the family, wife and children and others, may question what he says and take any initiative on their own. This kind of authority may even be passed on to the first born, if the first born is a male. The senior son may also exercise such absolute authority on his siblings -- brothers and sisters. The words "brothers" and "sisters" used in the African sense include cousins, nieces, and nephews in the extended family. It does not take much imagination to see the strong possibilities of children raised in such families growing up with developmental problems. Some of these could become passive aggressives.

In Africa, people are generally exposed to death of members of a family much earlier. The elaborate ritual ceremonies help members of the family to deal with the grief processes. However, there may be some cases where the grief process may not have been dealt with appropriately. One has in mind here the Christians who are at times confused about which rituals they can participate in. Others in this group may be the large numbers of urban dwellers, removed from the ethnic communities where they can deal with their griefs. These unresolved griefs and/or traumas may have influences on later behavior. In such cases, dealing with the behavior alone may be treating only the symptoms rather than the causes.

In some families, the man may have more than one wife and many children by the different women. In some of these houses, there is jealousy, bitterness, fighting, and quarreling. It may be hard for a child in such a family to appropriately actualize any of the eight stages of development by Erikson.

For the sake of those not familiar with Erikson's eight stages, a list and brief comments on them follow. These eight stages are Basic Trust vs. Basic Mistrust, Autonomy vs. Shame and Doubt, Initiative vs. Guilt, Industry vs. Inferiority, Identity vs. Identity Confusion, Intimacy vs. Isolation, Generativity vs. Stagnation, Integrity vs. Despair and Disgust.

(1) <u>Basic Trust vs. Basic Mistrust (Infancy)</u>

Basic trust is a quality acquired from the immediate family experience between child and parents. In this encounter, the child has both acquired and can exercise an appropriate reliability on others in the world around. It is an openness or perhaps a constrained openness or receptivity of others drawing upon the quality of receptivity from the child-parent encounter. This quality is not void of difficulties or frustrations, but it can still survive.[1] In an African society, the child learns to feel secure not just with father and mother but members of the extended family. Indeed, the child learns that members of the extended family also care for him/her.[2]

Basic mistrust is given birth in the child-parent encounter. This results in experiencing the world as unreliable, uncertain. The world and all that there is lacks some constancy and consistency.[3]

(2) <u>Autonomy vs. Shame and Doubt</u>

This is a period of development of the child, when he/she can exercise his/her power to grasp and let loose. The child experiences power within take, throw, assert, accept, or refuse.[4]

Shame and doubt seem to be the opposite sides of the coin of Autonomy. According to Capps, "...shame is the experience of being exposed to the disapproving gaze of the others. When subjected to excessive shaming, the child tends to develop greater inner rage or angry defiance of those doing the shaming."[5] Shame can be seen or is said to be expressed when there is "excessive self-control. Instead of learning to express our will in interaction with others, we stage interactions with others in advance, ensuring that these encounters are subject to neither variation nor chance."[6]

(3) Initiative vs. Guilt

Initiative is the ability to plan a strategy for how to do what. The child begins to gain more control of the body and direct moves. The child can walk, touch his eyes and ears, and walk to objects and places by his/her own will and power. The child can exercise aggression at a larger degree. Aggression is used here to mean power to move, to create, and to cause.

The opposite of initiative is the guilt feeling. At this stage "the child is unable to impose appropriate limits on this intrusiveness and thus becomes a 'transgressor.'"[7] There is a place for a natural curiosity in the exploration of this child, even if it is excessive. This curiosity becomes a problem only if it becomes too destructively aggressive and hostile. This may be traced to the parent-child and/or child-sibling rivalry or competition.[8]

(4) Industry vs. Inferiority

At this stage of the child's growth, he or she is capable of applying skills to tasks. In some societies in Africa, these range from taking care of siblings, fetching water, and cooking simple meals for girls and for boys, to taking care of animals or herds of the community. For those in school, they are capable of using simple tools. Generally, the tasks are industrious in nature. They achieve relative success in these tasks and win approval of the communities.

The opposite, inferiority, is felt if children at this stage cannot fulfill these tasks and subsequently, the approval of their community. Capps correctly points out that the inferiority "is also reflected in inhibitions due to an inadequate solution of conflicts from previous life stages."[9] Some of these inhibitions which result in inferiority may trace their source to the encounter of child and nucleus family and/or the extended family.

84

(5) Identity vs. Identity Confusion

This is the stage when the small individuality that has been asserting itself becomes one integrated individual. Individuality becomes unique and acknowledged as such by the individual. It is not an easy transition. It calls for intentionally coming to terms with one's understanding of who one is. Capps suggests that "...other selves beginning with our mothers in our infancy, help to shape and confirm this sense of being a center of awareness."[10]

This stage for most Africans means accepting one's societal roles. It may mean a readiness for a marriage life, for girls. It may also mean choosing/accepting one's goal in life in terms of a profession. The popular professions include teaching, farming, fishing, weaving, pottery making, carpentry, and business, to name a few.

Identity confusion is the opposite. The individual may not be integrated as a unique individual. The individual also does not have a clear sense of who he/she is and does not seem to be able to pursue an independent goal. The individual tends to be withdrawn and isolated.

(6) Intimacy vs. Isolation

This stage, like all the other stages, is dependent on the previous stage of Identity vs. Identity Confusion. For, to be intimate means risking identity, which makes one very vulnerable. It is dependent on the identity stage because intimacy at this stage is "involving letting this self go in order to form shared identities with others."[11] According to Capps this "may be due to a reluctance to abandon ourselves out of fear of self-loss, or to a need to repudiate other persons to our own."[12] Capps further offers an insight to the negative side that may be helpful for pastoral counseling. For Capps, the popular isolation includes the kind where a newly married couple slips into their own world. They almost cut connections with others in the world. Unfortunately, this tendency does not enhance their growth in intimacy "because it extends the self-protectiveness of the identity stage into the marriage relationship."[13]

(7) Generativity vs. Stagnation

This stage of development is one of the most important stages in Africa. Generativity as defined

85

by Capps "is concern for establishing and guiding the next generation."[14] In most African societies this may be the stage during which an individual engages in those acts that may qualify him/her to become an ancestor. This certainly includes raising a family. Another thing that one may engage in is striving for excellence in one's vocation. It also means being actively involved in the community affairs. It is also a period when one evaluates one's services or contributions to society. These are valued by the different ways the community bestows its recognition of the individual. In other words, one begins to take a leadership role and is being looked upon as a leader.

Stagnation is the opposite of generativity. It could be a very frustrating stage for an individual because of the emphasis on procreation and role patterns in most African communities. According to Capps, Erikson used stagnation to mean the loss or lack of inner drive or impetus to nurture. The individual engages in "self-absorption" which results in "stagnation and interpersonal impoverishments."[15] The individual, from an African perspective, may not only lack the driving force for generativity, but also may indeed be controlling it. Stagnation may have serious implications for the mental life of the individual; for he/she may be considered, in some societies in Africa, either to be cursed by the gods or as an extremely wicked person who must be feared. Hence, stagnation is an important clue for pastoral counselors to watch for.

(8) Integrity vs. Despair and Disgust

From an African perspective, this may be the stage where some people become living saints. They are heads of large families who preside over almost all family rituals. They may also become the custodians of the family property.

There are two levels of integrity. The first level is the one where an individual takes a long retrospective look at his life. In this retrospective vision, one takes note of those significant events and people one has encountered. In this process, one affirms one's self with gratitude for the quality of one's life. In some societies in Africa this sense of gratitude is incomplete or not realistic if it is not accompanied by a feeling of being on the way to join the ancestors with pride. In other words, one does not only accept one's life and death but celebrates them.

86

The second level is where one becomes proud of one's contribution to posterity by the number of children and grandchildren. There is also a feeling of successfully passing on the family traditions to posterity. In some cases, there are achievements of heroic acts in the community for which every member is proud of that individual.

The other side of the coin of Integrity is Despair and Disgust. What Capps describes about despair may be applicable to an African context. According to Capps, despair "...is often hidden behind a show of disgust, misanthropy, and contempt for other persons and institutions. There is also a self-contempt owing to little sense of comradeship with those whose lives and achievements mirror human dignity and love. This is a form of real disgust directed at oneself."16 This feeling of despair hidden behind disgust may be more evident when an individual compares himself/herself with mates of the same age who have rich and influential children and grandchildren. In modern Africa people look up to the families whose members are well educated and holding powerful and influential positions. In such families children give parents assistance like health facilities and money support.

The African Pastoral Counselor may have to become aware of these developmental factors.

The short lifespan in Africa due to malnutrition and lack of medical care is common knowledge. This may mean that some parents may die and leave their children in the care of relatives who may not always be impartial. Consequently, the children from such environments may grow up with developmental problems -- not feeling love and acceptance.

There is also the problem of divorces. A man or woman may divorce and leave the children with the spouse. The spouse may marry again and have children with the new spouse. Some of the dynamics in such families may sometimes have an effect on the development of the children.

The author believes that some of these developmental problems may need Freudian psychoanalysis with its intrapsychical emphasis. In such cases it may be that psychoanalysis can compliment or even supplement the kind of African therapy discussed so far.

In the dialogue between African therapy and the Persuasion and Healing Method, two helpful operative principles were identified. These are the notion of persuasion and the faith of the patient in the healer.

The persuasion principle may be helpful in increasing the qualitative effect of African therapy in a number of ways. It will make the African therapist more conscious of the dynamics of persuasion. The power of the unconscious and its subsequent damage to everyday encounters cannot be overemphasized.

If the therapist is conscious of his/her influence on the patient, it may result in a number of appropriate methods. The therapist should then be able to be conscious of his/her method of persuasion, and the subsequent effects of that method.

One danger of persuasion is projection. In an attempt to persuade someone to take a viewpoint, there may be subtle means of projecting the view of the therapist to the patient. It may be appropriate for the therapist to project, provided he/she is conscious that he/she is doing so and why it is done.

Projection also has the danger of not allowing the patient to tell his/her story. It is not uncommon for a therapist to be tempted to take over the patient's story and run it like his/hers. This may be especially true in cases where both therapist and patient may have similar experiences as husbands or wives, dealing with a marriage problem as widows or widowers, as orphans, or as a victim of one circumstance or another.

The notion of the faith of the patient toward the healer has a great deal of implication for the African therapist. It has both liabilities and potentials for healing. One of the liabilities is that it puts much responsibility on the therapist rather than the patient. In this regard, the therapist must be able to meet most of the expectations of the patient. The patient becomes a respondent instead of an initiator. It could also be abused by not taking seriously the psychological make-up of the patient. However, there is something to be said about the faith of the patient. Underneath the faith of the patient toward the therapist is the issue of trust.

Trust is a fundamental ingredient in any human development. An exploration of the trust element in a patient's faith may serve as a useful aspect of the therapy. In some cases, lack of trust could be the primary cause of the patient's problem.

It may be possible to say that the faith of the patient may also be a symptom of the developmental crisis of the patient.

88

These insights from psychoanalysis and the developmental theory of Erikson may enhance African therapy and consequently be integrated into the practice of pastoral counseling in Africa.

ENDNOTES

1.   Donald Capps, <u>Life Cycle Theory and Pastoral Care</u>, edited by Don Browning, (Philadelphia: Fortress Press, 1983), p. 24.

2.   Esther L. Megil, <u>Education in the African Church</u>, (London: Geoffrey Chapman, 1981), p. 16.

3.   Capps, p. 24.

4.   Ibid., p. 25.

5.   Ibid.

6.   Ibid.

7.   Ibid.

8.   Ibid.

9.   Ibid., p. 26.

10.   Ibid., p. 27.

11.   Ibid., p. 28.

12.   Ibid.

13.   Ibid.

14.   Ibid.

15.   Ibid.

16.   Ibid., p. 30.

Chapter 7

Models for African Pastoral Counseling

I. Introduction

It is possible to conclude that the kind of African therapy described in the previous chapter is a community affair. It can be called social therapy. In other words, the therapy for the individual is derived from the social drama. This seems different from psychoanalysis as outlined earlier. It probably looks absurd to Western psychologists, analysts, or therapists. However, it could be that this difference, when explored, will enrich Africans and westerners and other cultures. Such an effort is being attempted by some Africans. The author is only joining in that effort.

In this chapter, the social context of African therapy will be taken seriously. It may appear that the author is a member of the school of social psychology from an African perspective. The author wishes neither to be a schoolist nor to be categorized. If anything, he belongs to the African therapist group. Hence, the data provided by African societies is a starting point. There are two reasons that make the African social data attractive to the author:

(1) The author believes that the African societies communicate much about what goes on in the lives of the individual within the society. (2) It is in the society that therapy is most effective. The community in many ways reflects the conflicts and it is the community or society that offers therapy.

The society's systems of communication, verbal and nonverbal, are imperative sources of data for pastoral counselors. The author strongly believes that African communities constantly manifest both the objective and subjective realities of individuals. Therefore, the language of the communities is necessary for the models of pastoral counseling that will be proposed further. To do this effectively, the discussion will be informed partly by the treatise of The Social Construction of Reality by Berger and Luckman.[1]

Berger and Luckman draw from the field of developmental psychology for their theory. Most developmental psychologists believe that the infant does not have notions or sense of differentiation. Indeed, the infant at birth does not even differentiate between the mother and the self.

It is the community that introduces names, and meanings of objects to the infant.[2] According to Crescimanno, "the emergence of the sense of self in the individual is interplay between the biological and social dimensions of the human organism."[3] For Crescimanno, language is indispensable for basic understanding of the self. To be able to articulate one's identity, one will need to use words.[4] Crescimanno therefore suggests that "words as labels are generally the carriers of meaning, which is why people are so dependent upon them in relating to and knowing the world."[5]

As an analogy, Crescimanno further suggests that language can be compared to the building blocks used to build a house. Language then as blocks is used to build a "house of one's consciousness."[6] Crescimanno also drew from Mead's notion of symbolic interaction and the labeling perspective.[7] Crescimanno, appropriating Berger, suggests that the gap between the individual and the society is bridged by a process of socialization. It is in these processes of socialization that "meanings are constructed, maintained and transformed through the symbolic interaction."[8]

Symbolic interaction is not an inherent quality. It is a process that does not take place in a vacuum but "within the social context of concrete, recognizable, and labeled social surroundings."[9]

The world as socially constructed is a way of ordering, of interpreting experience and giving meanings. According to Berger, a meaningful order or nomos, "is imposed upon the concrete experiences and meanings of individuals."[10] The process of ordering is what Berger refers to as nomizing activity.[11] The role of language in nomizing is to impose "differentiation and structure upon ongoing influx of experience."[12] In the process of nomizing, language also builds "up cognitive and normative edifice that passes for 'knowledge' in a society."[13]

Forms of Communication in an African Therapy

For many Africans, philosophy may not be constructing ideas and concepts in abstract terms. Life is not a dualism or any such division. Both past and future events have influences on the present. The present and future also have influences on the past and of course the past and present have a big influence in the future.

For some African communities, everyday life manifests concrete reality. So they do derive much meaning from the realities of everyday life. It may be "subjectively meaningful to them as a coherent world."14

What they may interpret and appropriate as meaningful in these communities may be empirical but not necessarily scientific. The fact that it may not be scientific has caused some to doubt the validity of such claims. But then it is common knowledge that not all scientific claims are absolutes. In some cases, they are contradictory. A common example is the motion of light in waves and also in straight lines. To help conceptualize divination as a kind of therapy and an important source of data, this discussion will be limited to everyday forms of communication in some African communities.

II. **Language**

Language "with necessary objectifications posits the order within which [everyday experiences] make sense"15 for all humans. It does not matter whether that language is verbal or nonverbal, whether it consists of moans and groans or click sounds. In many African communities, the reality of their experiences in everyday life communication is very obvious. It does not always need scientific verification. Hence, the scientific verification with all its biases may not be deemed necessary. However, it does not mean that what they see as reality may not be verified or cannot be verified. Hence in most African communities, "the reality of everyday life further presents itself to [them] as an intersubjective world, a world that [they] share with others."16

The common language of these communities for objectification of their experiences is based "on everyday life and keeps pointing back to it as [they] employ it to interpret experiences in finite provinces of meaning."17 Berger and Luckman may be right when they say "human expressivity is capable of objectivation. Such objectivations serve as more or less enduring indices of the subjective processes of their producers, allowing their availability to extend beyond the face-to-face situation."18 This quote seems to provide important insight to understanding the kind of therapy used in divination.

For example, a situation of misunderstanding between members of the family may lead to death.

The descendants may enact the anger in the therapy with the therapist by referring to a spear. The spear helps the patient to dramatize that anger. The subjective or repressed anger is objectified by the spear.

The spear is an object that symbolizes both defense as in war and also attack either in war with a neighbor or when hunting an animal for food. At the divination, it is more than just a symbol of these. It is a sign of anger for the patient; the anger that may have created anxiety, perhaps even psychosomatic illness. This anger may be dramatized here. This may be how the Tallensis dramatize and evoke the experience powerfully and meaningfully for effective therapy.

The diviner may be humming a song. It is also common knowledge that music has the power to induce emotions. The diviner also has two metals and other objects including a spear, the beard of a goat, and the feet of other animals. In the course of singing, he hits the metals with the wand (piece of stick) while the patient is holding the lower half of the stick. He hits the metals, points to the beard which may normally be a symbol of maleness but at that stage has acquired a sign of the image of the patient's father or relative who died violently. He hits the metal again and hums, points to the beard, hits again, points to the spear, hits and hits as he hums.

The message that is brought face to face or the subjective drama now objectified in the face-to-face encounter here is simple to deduce without any profound knowledge of Tallensis divination. A male had a confrontation with another male. This resulted in violent confrontation. The therapist may hit a hoe which may mean an instrument for farming, so he may be suggesting that they fought violently over land. He hits, again and again. This could probably evoke weeping. He points to an object with red color, which may mean blood was shed. He hits the spear again, again, and again which may mean anger, violence, destruction.

As suggested by Berger and Luckman, the spear "...has become an objective constituent of the reality"[19] of the family feud. The spear now expresses a "subjective intention of violence...and an objectivation of human subjectivity."[20] It is therefore possible to suggest that everyday life for some African communities is real and a source of therapy, because they "serve as [indices] of subjective meanings."[21] The form of communication with language, drama, and symbols as suggested by Berger and Luckman is "capable of becoming [indeed are] the objective repository of vast accumulations of meaning and experience of...can..then preserve in time and transmit to following generations.22 Therefore, the social reality of everyday life in Africa can provide important therapeutic resources for the ministry of counseling.

The challenge is thrown to students of pastoral theology by Africa through the words of Mosala. Mosala attempts to explain the South African situation of the Blacks and the enormous task of pastoral care and counseling in South Africa. He argues rather convincingly that the Blacks' system of counseling, which used to be available to the individuals through extended family throughout one's stages in life, is being destroyed by unique problems of South Africa, and mass adaptation of inappropriate Western models of counseling. This may be a problem for Africa in general. The problem may not just be the fact that these models started in the West. The problem may be that these models may not have been critically evaluated to determine their suitability or nonsuitability. Further, there may not be any attempt to integrate them into an African system of counseling.

The situation of counseling is made more difficult in South Africa by the uprooting of families, violences on families, and satanic, inhumane, apartheid policies. Mosala makes a compelling case with two examples. In one case, a black couple went to a government-subsidized, family counseling service, headed by a White. The counseling was to be carried out by two white students in clinical psychology. The two students asked that the session be recorded by both tape and video. Of course, the couple objected. While one may appreciate the students' need to record it in order to get help to improve their skills,23 one must also bear in mind that in a white recording anything done or said by a Black evokes great fears on the part of the Black. When politics becomes inseparably connected with counseling, pastoral counseling is distorted, and consequently may lose its vital function in a community.

In another case, an old lady tells a priest her dream which is of some significant concern to her. In her dream she is told that her cup will not be blessed for not knowing the secrets of the Catholic Church. The priest listens, gives some few words of advice, gives her a blessing, and continues his task of trying to give communion to as many people as possible.24

It may be tempting to blame the priest of being insensitive or uncaring. The priest may have been insensitive. The real problem for the priest may be that he has not been sufficiently prepared in counseling. One does not have to be a Freudian or Jungian analyst to be available to people. However, in most African countries, theological training does not adequately prepare ministers/priests or even concretely provide them with the very basic skills of caring and being with those who need some help. One learns these in the field. The sad fact for Africa is that seminarians are not made aware of the resources available within the culture and the society in order to learn from them.

These resources include some of the old men and women who have been doing caring and counseling for years and have acquired a wealth of experience. Some resources also include tales, music, and dance. Their normal, everyday aspects of life may sometimes be taken for granted. One cannot help but take seriously the challenge of Mosala that "In the third world there is a crying need for us to take a deep look at the very things we sometimes dismiss as trivial and meaningless. Scholars who study these issues do not seem keen to go beyond studying and describing [to provide] new...models for actions."[25] In an attempt to respond to this cry and challenge, the following models are offered.

It is hoped that in these models of counseling, the patients will come to understand themselves better and relate appropriately to their sociocultural cosmos. The objective here is that change will be effected in behavior. This will subsequently help patients to act more responsibly toward themselves, their family, and their world.

As already indicated, African therapy aims at integration into society. Consequently, these models may be able to "increase the client's repertory of roles and his ability to play a single role more fully."[26] These models may also be able to heal those who may have developed a "rigid pattern of behavior." They may also offer the "rigid patterned" a larger margin of flexibility in behavior in interaction and enable them to face issues with courage.

In Africa where roles such as sons, daughters, fathers, mothers, and uncles are important, these models have some significant values. These models have potential in helping those in these roles "...express a range of emotions, think a range of thoughts, perform a range of actions...within the boundaries of that role.[27] These models also try to use the symbols of language and music, movement, images, and feelings of the individual concerned.

Landy may be helpful when he says:

> In applying these devices to drama therapy, the therapist uses the stylization as a distancing device which can reveal the actual needs and problems of the client....the therapist works to help the client view the dialectic between mask and the face, the persona and the person.[28]

This point is expanded in the author's first volume.

These devices of language, music, images, and movement help patients to examine the different facets of their existence that will make conscious the "dialectical, posed between the life of imagination, the fictional, the subjective, and the life of the everyday, the actual, the objective."[29]

These models in many ways are able to integrate ritual into therapy most effectively. Rituals play an important role in African therapy. So therapy may be said to be incomplete without any form or kind of ritual in Africa.

Ritual as defined by Landy "is a symbolic action repeated in a prescribed way to perpetuate the status, to affirm a common bond among members of a community and to defend an individual or group against danger."[30]

It can be compared to theatrical acts or drama in the way ritual is practiced in Ghana and many African countries. One could agree with Landy's suggestion that "ritual activity thus is dramatic, as it calls for the subject to create a representational world through symbolic means."[31]

Divination, an African therapy, does perform this function in its therapeutic role. In this regard, African therapists use rituals with individuals and communities to stage "ritual dramas that embody themes and supernatural characters representing the collective concerns of the group."[32] Rituals may also help the patient to release some repressed emotions by means of catharsis.[33] According to Landy, ritual is a form of drama therapy, because of its potential to "combine healing and performance and proceed through acts of imagination."[34] Rituals are also effective in drama therapy because they enable the patient to suspend his doubt and take part in the drama. The advantage for the patient is that he/she can

97

experience "a greater sense of release and integration."[35] This point is alluded to in the discussion of the Persuasion and Healing Method.

In an African context, this could mean that the patient has now become fully knitted into the community. The solidarity and sense of oneness is restored. It further means the community can expect regular rains, good harvest. They will also get more babies. Indeed, they will experience "Shalom." These models therefore could be effective therapeutic tools for pastoral counselors in Africa.

ENDNOTES

1.   Peter L. Berger and Thomas Luckman, <u>The Social Construction of Reality: A Treatise in the Sociology of Knowledge</u>, (Garden City, N.Y.: Doubleday & Co., Inc., 1966).

2.   Ibid.

3.   Russel Crescimanno, <u>Culture, Consciousness, and Beyond: An Introduction</u>, (New York: University Press of America, Inc., 1982), p. 16.

4.   Ibid.

5.   Ibid., p. 19.

6.   Ibid.

7.   George H. Mead, <u>Mind, Self and Society</u>, (Chicago: University of Chicago Press, 1956).

8.   Crescimanno, p. 20.

9.   Ibid., p. 21.

10.   Peter L. Berger, <u>The Sacred Canopy</u>, (Garden City, N.Y.: Doubleday & Co., Inc., 1967), p. 19.

11.   Ibid., p. 19.

12.   Ibid.

13.   Ibid.

14.   Berger and Luckman, p. 19.

15.   Ibid., p. 22.

16.   Ibid., p. 23.

17.   Ibid., p. 26.

18.   Ibid., p. 34.

19.   Ibid., p. 35.

20.   Ibid.

21.   Ibid.

22.   Ibid., p. 37.

23.   Bernadette I. Mosala, "Pastoral Care and Family Counselling: South African Experience" in Mosamba Ma Mpolo and Cecile De Sweemer (ed.) <u>Families in Transition</u> (Geneva: W.C.C., 1987).

24.   Ibid., p. 86.

25.   Ibid., p. 86-87.

26.   Robert J. Landy, <u>Drama Therapy: Concepts and Practices</u>, (Springfield, Ill.: Charles C. Thomas Publisher, 1986), p. 44.

27.   Ibid., p. 45.

28.   Ibid., p. 47.

29.   Ibid., p. 48.

30.   Ibid., p. 67.

31.   Ibid.

32.   Ibid., p. 69.

33.   Ibid.

34.   Ibid.

35.   Ibid.

III. Storytelling

Storytelling, like dance and music, is part of the psychodrama of everyday life in Africa. Psychodrama denotes the idea of playing out psychological concepts in drama or activities. At times, the people are aware of the psychological ideas or concepts imparted. At other times, they are not. Africans have transmitted their myths of life to posterity by way of stories and proverbs since time immemorial. Indeed, storytelling is an important part of oral tradition. It could be called an educational tool.

Storytelling in Africa usually is intended to convey or transmit history, or provide wisdom-moral guidance for formation of character. Some of the stories are for aetiological purposes, when no empirical data can adequately explain a phenomenon, such as why humans die. Other stories are religious as well. In almost all African communities, there are stories that attempt to give meaningful answers to such questions as how humans came to the world, the world in relation to God -- often called the myth of creation and fall. There are also stories of people of supernatural wisdom, which in Akan is symbolized in anansi and in Tallensis, sambula.

The mythical figure of anansi or sambula is invariably wisest, with no equal in the community. He communicates with humans but is more than human. He always knows what to do, when, and how. His power is to be appreciated but not envied. If one dares become competitive with anansi or sambula, one is bound to fail miserably and the consequent shame is unbearable.

There are also some stories that psychodramatize the conflicts of parents and children, husbands and wives, humans and nature, to name a few.

Other stories psychodramatize the insecurities, anxieties, and fears of various occupations in the communities, such as fishermen, farmers, hunters, weavers, and diviners, to list a few.

Most African people tell stories in the evening over an intergenerational fireplace. By the fire, the wisdom of the elderly is transmitted to the younger generations in stories. The author dares to suggest that the fire sessions are the oldest form of African academies. Some of these provided entertainment as well as religious instruction.

Some African stories have motifs. For example, Beier is of the opinion that "African storytellers and mythmakers have shown their ingenuity and inventiveness in uncountable stories in which they have

101

explained the origin of death."[1] Beier, in his book, compiles different stories from different parts of Africa that reflect different aspects of life in Africa.

Barker and Sinclair may have been ahead of their time in their lamentation that the introduction of western civilization may destroy the rich tradition and valuable means of preservation and transmission of values. Commenting on the fast expansion of western civilization, they said, it "tends to be fatal to the mythology, the customs and the traditions of such peoples as the Negroes of West Africa."[2] They gathered stories from people from the rural areas. The stories in this book, mostly from Ghana, reflect the morals, the occupations, and wisdom, etc., of Ghanaians.

Jan Knappert also compiled many stories from Kenya. It would seem that Knappert had a religious interest, so he tried to give either some Christian-biased interpretations or direct interpolations to these stories. He tries in each story to indicate either an implied Judeo-Christian notion or a direct correspondence to such a notion. Unfortunately, Knappert seems to exercise so much of his thematic control and interest that some of the stories may lose their original context.[3]

The other objection to the book is the title, Myths and Legends from Swahili. There is no tribe in Africa called Swahili. Swahili is a common-denominator, official language of communication. So one cannot get a myth and legend from such a language. Probably, he may be referring to the ethnic communities these tales and myths came from rather than the synthetic language called Swahili.

Susan Feldmann, in her book, compiled African myths and tales.[4] She categorized them into two parts. Part one is her category of myths of primeval times -- beginnings, origins of death. In part two, she calls them tales. These include trickster tales, explanatory tales, dilemma stories with morals, and tales of human adventure.

These "myths" and "tales" are drawn from different parts of Africa. What this author objects to about her approach is that she analyzes these stories as one would a Shakespearian tale. One cannot help but question how she can attempt explanations of all these stories from different parts of Africa.

Storytelling is an old art in Africa and is very helpful as a tool for counseling. One powerful use of storytelling is captured most in a little book published by the World Council of Churches that contains stories of women as seen in the light of the Gospel. In this book, these women want to share their experiences. The women learn that "painful as some of our stories were, they seemed like gifts to help us grow in sensitivity towards 'bent-over' people."5

Hillman as a depth psychologist makes some comments on the benefits of a story. He posits that to have story awareness is by itself psychologically therapeutic. For Hillman, to have stories told to one at childhood is preferable.

He suggests it comes with life and "is a perspective of life."6 Hillman further suggests that the unconscious serves as a container of stories. It may be these stories, in the unconscious that help individuals to organize events and derive meaning from them.7

Stories for Hillman "are means of finding one's self in events that may not otherwise make psychological sense."8 Healing in analysis may be effective because one is able to put all disturbing experiences into a story.9 Hillman makes some observations that may be important for rapidly westernizing Africa to hear. For Hillman, not every kind of story needs to be told. He prefers stories that are of the culture, namely Greek, Roman, Celtic, and Nordic myths, the Bible, legends, and tales.10

The criticisms of Hillman's view must also be noted. It is argued by those of rationalist and associationist theory of mind that if children were not introduced to such tales in their early years, they could have less pathology and more rationality when they grow.11 He objects that the above allegation does not agree with his observation in many years of practice. He rather argues that "through the story, the symbolic quality of pathological images and themes are less likely to be viewed naturalistically...These images find legitimate places in story."12 He therefore concludes that "story awareness provides a better way than clinical awareness for coming to terms with one's own case history."13 Storytelling thus viewed, may be a very important orientation of mind, character, and personality formation. It could also be preparing resources as coping mechanisms in later life for individuals within the culture.

Storytelling in many ways has the power to unite people for the simple reason that other people's stories intersect with us and ours also intersect with them. Stories also have the potential of connecting individuals to their culture. As rightly observed by Bausch, "every people, nation, and community have stories and myths that preserve and prolong the traditions that give them their identity."[14] Apart from the larger community to which an individual belongs, every individual, especially in Africa, belongs to a clan and a small community which "also have their identifying stories that link them to who they are, to their culture."[15]

It has also been pointed out that stories have a special language that help an individual to get in touch with the unconscious. This is best shown by nightmare talk in dreams. Nightmare talk brings the images and fantasies into the unconscious. According to Bausch, "these images express our deepest selves and the experience of the sacred that is embedded in that psychological unity."[16]

Many stories effect healing because they at times afford an opportunity to relive a past experience, the effect of which is still present. They also provide hope for the hopeless. When one finds oneself in difficulties, stories of people in similar situations stir imaginations to other alternatives.[17]

Finally Bausch suggests that stories help humans express their experiences of paradoxes of life. Some of these paradoxes include spirituality rooted in earthiness, the knowing of the absolute freedom in disobedience, triumph growing out of suffering, security found in uncertainty, and prayer in study.[18]

Implication for Counseling

Stories as tools for counseling seem to be one of the natural ways for most, if not all, of Africa. Using stories does require techniques but it certainly does not require that the counselor necessarily ought to be either a Freudian or Jungian analyst. As suggested earlier, many theories articulated by western psychoanalysts and psychotherapists such as Freud and Jung echo elements in many African life practices long before Freud and Jung were born. In the African scene, Mpolo seems to be the one, as far as the author knows, who has consciously taken stories as tools of counseling seriously. It is common knowledge that the African therapists use these but only a few have tried to interpret them in some systematized form. It is very necessary, indeed imperative, that stories be used in African pastoral counseling.

Storytelling may offer the opportunity for an authentic African pastoral theology of healing and wholeness. In the light of this objective, stories could be looked at as a model of pastoral counseling.

It is probably appropriate to state here a method by which stories could be used in counseling. There are many ways, but the author can only suggest one and leave the rest to the creativity and ingenuity of African counselors.

If it is uncertain how to begin a session, a story could be used. It could be from either the counselor or the counselee, preferably from the counselee. The counselee could tell a story. There are four levels of using the story: 1) The language could be a source of identification. In language, the words used could mean something for the counselee. 2) The role of the characters of the story could also provide something for the counselee. 3) The mood of the story as a whole and of the individual characters in particular may also become important sources of insight. 4) The context of the story -- whether it was a home, market, school, or farm -- could also be an important element for the counselee and for the session.

Some people develop problems because of the way they interpret reality. How they interpret the everyday life reality may blur their experiences, and this interpretation in many ways poses limits on them physically, mentally, spiritually, and socially. The influences of how they interpret reality may be deeply rooted in the early stage of their lives.

They may develop what the psychologists call psychopathology. Psychopathology as used here means an earlier experience or encounter that has a negative influence on later behavior and/or perception. The individual may be unaware of the impact of this negative influence that sets a pattern of behavior. As indicated earlier, some of the causes of psychopathology may have their roots in the early stages of life encounters.

These earlier encounters did not enhance growth; rather they had a negative effect and retarded emotional and/or spiritual growth. These events or incidents or influences may have been traumatic in some cases. For others they developed slowly into a "dysfunctional representational system."19 These negative effects tend to lead to or subsequently cause the development of other kinds of problems. So it is difficult at times to tell which caused what and when.

Many people have speculated about the first cause and attempted to remove that initial blockage in order to address the root cause rather than concentrate on symptoms or later problems primarily caused by the first early childhood experience.

It seems the first cause theory underlies Freudian psychoanalysis. He thought that many of these early blockages were caused by early traumas in childhood. For Freud, "The trauma was not an historical act or even an influence. It traces its roots not to a mode of interpreting and responding to reality, but one's subjective experience including the most fanciful interpretations of actual events."[20]

His solution to the problem was to gain "insight into the forgotten experiences and shared this with the patient."[21] This should straighten up the individual and relieve him/her of emotional trauma.[22] Unfortunately, it did not work with all of his patients. Indeed, he found out that even when he gained the insight, sharing it with the patient was one of the times he experienced the most resistance.[23] One can only agree with the observation by Hoffman that "an intellectualist view of the situation was clearly inadequate."[24]

This may be where an African understanding of stories and subsequent use for counseling may be adequate in dealing with cases of this kind in Africa. For purposes of analysis of African therapy, the social construction of reality was used.

As a follow-up to that theory, one would say that for some Africans, history is not just a chronology of facts and figures but of experiences. Therefore, most stories Africans tell are not just for entertainment but also reflect historical experiences individually and collectively.

For example, one story from a hunting community recounts a time of a man and his son who went game hunting. The man and son lose each other. Unfortunately, the father goes home, leaving the son behind. Alone, tired, hungry and thirsty, almost face to face with his death, he hears a bird singing. He imitates the noise of the bird. Somehow the bird seems to wait on him while it flies in a direction. He follows the bird to a river and gets some water to drink. While resting, some people come. He follows them and returns home safely but with anger and resentment against his father.

When telling the story, the hunter may imitate the singing of the bird, perhaps the style of flying of the bird. The other people listening may be amused and think his movement absurd. The young hunter sees in this story more than entertainment. In it he recalls the anger against his father but gratitude to mother nature who provided a bird.

This story may also affect the community's understanding of the cordial relationship with nature and the dilemma of depending on nature -- game -- for livelihood and survival. The drama in this story may symbolize some images of the bird as a totem, or earlier experiences of not being wanted by the father or not being cared for, which may have been suppressed in the unconscious at this time.

In the case of the story retold, a counselor will have to creatively work with this story in order to effect "a change in [the hunter's] basic understanding of self and world...with a modification in the memories which are a vehicle for that understanding."25 A pastoral counselor in Africa may use this story and help the counselee reflect on the events of the story in detail, the parts of the story that he identifies most with his experience -- the sense of estrangement, the loss or lack of filial and parental bond.

Ira Progoff makes an instructive observation about the relationship between stories and counseling. Stories we tell "draw our life into focus so that we have a basis for making decisions...that give us a perspective of the pattern and context of our life as a whole, [they enable] us to have an inner perspective of the movement of our life."26 Even though Progoff made these observations with reference to daily journals, stories for most Africans serve a similar function.

The use of stories reflecting actual events as a form of a healing method has long been a kind of therapy in Africa. The elders used them in funerals and for other special occasions.

Most traditional African tales open themselves up to different interpretations and meanings. This quality may help to make them better therapeutic tools because they can reach individuals and communities at different levels without exhaustion. This is best illustrated by some of the creation myths. They are both different in different communities and familiar. The quality of stories alluded to here may be the power of their paradoxes.

The so-called fairy tales in Africa could be good tools to be used to explore the sociological, cultural, and religious perspective accompanied by some inherent psychological insights. They could be means to a way into the inner world of the individual.[27] In a sense one could say they are the objectification of the intersubjectivity. In the story of the hunter just told, this story is "a form of vicarious experience."[28]

This story affords an African counselor an opportunity to explore with the counselee the characters and feelings in the story that have their counterparts in his life in a nonthreatening way that would have been difficult otherwise. The drama in the story also adds another important advantage because drama "capture basic insights into human existence and models for human behavior."[29] It may be possible in this story to unearth or bring to light some other previous hurts from neglect on the part of the father. The son may not have been aware of the hurts; nonetheless, they were there and could have had an effect in the dramatization of the story.

Robert Hobson, a Jungian-influenced analyst, has used stories in family therapy. From that experience he observes that a therapist could employ "cultural analogies...sometimes cast in the form of stories...to supply information which is new to the patient but which is relevant to his [her] present problem, within and without the therapeutic interview."[30]

Hoffman, commenting on Hobson's use of the story, makes a helpful addition. He adds that "the use of story in family therapy [counseling] avoids exclusively intellectual patterns of comprehension, allowing each member of the family to his or her own appropriation of the narrative."[31]

It is possible that the use of story may help the counselor to glimpse where the client is, the client's understanding of the situation in relation to the problem, and some ideas of what his/her goal may be based on. As suggested by Hoffman, intellectual abstractions tend to increase resistance.

Use of stories could reduce the anxiety level. It probably also gives a healthy start. Usually, the characters they role play in the story and the dynamics of those roles in many cases have some relevance to the real life situation of the counselee.

In some stories, some coping mechanisms that the counselee could draw on are implied. In others, the coping mechanism may not be there or it is not appropriate and other alternatives need to be explored. In a case where the counselee identifies with a certain role, it may be helpful to suggest role-reversal. The counselee may be able to get some understanding from experiencing both perspectives. The role-reversal does have a potential of altering the counselee's usual way of interpreting the dynamics of the situation from his/her perspective only. This approach "may not be to give a model for behavior, or to offer a path to success within the already accepted context, but rather to disrupt that whole vision which opens the way for radically new thinking."32

Myths and Proverbs

Some aspects of myths are alluded to in the section about storytelling. This is only a brief outline of the therapeutic value of myths in Africa.

Myths have mostly been studied from two perspectives: 1) the internal content of myths, and 2) the place of myths in the lives of people in African communities. The former concerns mostly literary critics while the latter concerns mostly anthropologists and historians.[33] A myth by the definition of Barbour "is a story which is taken to manifest some aspect of the cosmic order."[34]

Myths offer some glimpses of the loose but basic structure of reality. "The present is interpreted in the light of the formative events narrated in the myth..."[35]

Barbour further quotes Berger as referring to myth as "ordering of experience as 'nomizing' encosmizing the adoption of a dramatized cosmic framework of human experience."[36]

As in storytelling, drama, and music, myths deal with important everyday experiences that may be "perennial problems and the enduring order of the world in which man [including Africans] lives."[37] Myths also help Africans in their search to claim their identity. An African generally takes the past serious. One's relationship to land, to a political position, to a religious rite is mostly determined by one's past.

What Barbour writes about community in general is particularly true of Africa. "A community is constituted by the key events which it remembers and in which its members participate."[38] In most African communities myths are alive. They are alive in a sense that they "evoke personal involvement rather than contemplation or conceptual analysis."[39] Myths set a process whereby the individual member of a community may be interpreted in the community and the cosmos order.

Myths also provide the link between humans and the cosmic order.[40] Some myths in Africa also express a Salvific notion of life. These are shown in Feldman's works on African myths and tales cited in the section dealing with storytelling. In most of the myths of creation, there was a perfect state of being quite different from where and how things are now. From the myth comes an explanation of how people lost or distorted the state. As suggested by Barbour, "myths thus portray and convey a power to transform

110

man's life, rather than a predominantly theoretical explanation of it."[41] Many examples of these kinds of myths are found in Jan Knappert's book Myths and Legends from Swahili.

Myths offer patterns or models for humans to imitate. This is even true for myths that deal with religious truths or qualities worth imitating. It is this power in myths that enables them "...to fix the paradigmatic models for all rites and significant activities -- eating, sexuality, work, education, etc. Myths are vividly impressive, inspiring their adherents to emotional response and concrete action."[42] The notion of myths in the above understanding may partly explain why most rituals in Africa have their origin in myths rather than analytical concepts or scientific theories.

The Functions of Myths

The functions of myths will be limited to the psychosocial and psychoreligious. The psychosocial perspectives may be "symbolic disguises" and "elaborations." In this way, they can "satisfy insistent emotional needs without appearing to do so blatantly."[43] As further suggested by Schneiderman, myths "in psychodynamics terms communicate unconscious wishes or fears expressed as miraculous stories."[44]

Myths in most African communities may also serve as explanations for rituals. Schneiderman furthermore offers an explanation that myths and ritual reinforce each other. While myth attempts to explain ritual, rituals may also reinforce the collective identity and interdependence of the community. By this dialectic relationship, myths may channel the anxiety of the individual, provide a community basis for the support.[45] In a ritual, anxiety may be at least reduced "by the use of sympathetic magic or by sacrificial acts."[46]

Myths in most African communities may also attempt to bridge psychologically the distances existing in creation or the universe. They may also seek to bring together both the human and spirit worlds. They try to bring together the opposite poles of "alienation" and "integration" "by calling to mind a fabulous history of past encounters between the humans and the superhuman, between the divine and the demonic, or between magical animals and the natural order."[47]

Myths may further attempt to teach humans that the world as they see it predates them and is part of a whole beyond humans. Myths may seek to give a deeper meaning to human experience.

Social Functions of Myths

Since Durkheim, many scholars have written on the theme of the social functions of myths. Myths in most African communities have an integrating and unifying power. They also attempt to keep both individuals and community in harmony.

Myths in some cases may not only create social order but also try to order it and provide basic explanations for the existence and running of social, political, and cultural institutions. Myths which deal with morals and value systems perform this function most. The myths of morality or value systems cannot be analyzed as true or wrong. Myths may be a basic guide. The cognitive elements of myth must be cautiously pursued. Alasdair MacIntyre makes some helpful observations in this regard. He writes: "A myth is living or dead, not true or false. You cannot refute a myth because as soon as you treat it as refutable, you do not treat it as a myth but as a hypothesis or history."[48]

One can appropriately ask the question, what truths do myths have? For Barbour, "...they would be valid in so far as they authentically express man's feelings, hopes and fears or his experiences of guilt, reconciliation and liberation from anxiety."[49] Carl Jung develops the notion of myths in more detail. For Jung, myths are very important in the understanding of the psychological development of persons. Jung sees myths as symbols that express the intrapsychical dynamics within a person and a culture. He maintains that

> for the analogies between ancient myths and the stories that appear in the dreams of modern patients are neither trivial nor accidental. They exist because the unconscious minds of modern man preserve the symbol-making capacity that once found expression in the beliefs and rituals of the primitive.[50]

According to Jung, the symbol-making ability has a psychic importance. These symbols carry important messages that influence the attitude and behaviors of humans.[51]

It can be implied from Jung's understanding that it is imperative for pastoral counselors in Africa to understand the symbols of their people. The better they understand these symbols the more effective

112

their counseling could be. It can be implied by Jung's suggestion that the link between primitive myths and the unconscious may help counselors and counselees "...to identify and to interpret these symbols in a context that gives them historical perspective and psychological meaning."52

ENDNOTES

1.   Ulli Beier (ed.), <u>The Origin of Life and Death - African Creation Myths</u>, (London: Heinemann, 1969), p. ix.

2.   W.H. Barker and Cecilia Sinclair, <u>West African Folk Tales</u>, (London: George A. Harrup & Co., 1917), p. 13.

3.   Jan Knappert, <u>Myth and Legends of Swahili</u>, (London: Heinemann Educational Books, 1970).

4.   Susan Feldman, <u>African Myths and Tales</u>, (New York: Dell Publishers Co., Inc., 1963).

5.   <u>By Our Lifes -- Stories of Women Today and in the Bible</u>, (Geneva: W.C.C., 1985), p. xiv.

6.   James Hillman, "A Note On Story" in <u>Parabola</u>, vol. IV, No. 4, Nov. 1979, p. 43.

7.   Ibid.

8.   Ibid.

9.   Ibid., p. 44.

10.   Ibid., p. 45.

11.   Ibid., p. 43.

12.   Ibid.

13.   Ibid.

14.   William J. Bausch, <u>Story Telling: Imagination and Faith</u>, (Mystic, Connecticut: Twenty-third Publications, 1984), p. 33.

15.   Ibid.

16.   Ibid., p. 38.

17.   Ibid., p. 61.

18.   Ibid., p. 65ff.

19.   John C. Hoffman, <u>Law, Freedom and Story: The Role Of Narrative In Therapy, Society And Faith</u>, (Waterloo, Canada: Wilfrid Laurier University Press, 1986), p. 41.

20.   Ibid.

21.   Ibid.

22.   Ibid.

23.   Ibid.

24. Ibid.

25. Ibid., p. 42.

26. Ira Progoff, <u>At A Journal Workshop</u>, (New York: Dialogue House Library, 1975), p. 98-99.

27. Hoffman, p. 46.

28. Ibid., p. 47.

29. Ibid.

30. Ibid.

31. Ibid., p. 49.

32. Ibid., p. 53.

33. Ian G. Barbour, <u>Myths, Models and Paradigms</u>, (New York: Harper & Row Publisher, 1974).

34. Ibid., p. 20.

35. Ibid.

36. Ibid.

37. Ibid.

38. Ibid.

39. Ibid.

40. Ibid.

41. Ibid., p. 21.

42. Ibid., p. 19.

43. Leo Schneiderman, <u>The Psychology of Myth, Folklore and Religion</u>, (Chicago: Nelson-Hall, 1981), p. 187.

44. Ibid.

45. Ibid., p. 189.

46. Ibid., p. 192.

47. Ibid., p. 196.

48. Alasdair MacIntyre, "Myth" in P. Edward (ed.) <u>Encyclopedia of Philosophy</u>, vol. 5., p. 435.

49. Barbour, p. 25.

50.   Carl A. Jung, M.L. Von Franz, Joseph L. Henderson, Jolande Jacobi, Ariele Jaffe, <u>Man and His Symbols</u>, (New York: Dell Publishing Co., Inc., 1968), p. 98.

51.   Ibid.

52.   Ibid., p. 100.

IV. Dance and Drama

Dance, in all of its forms and kinds, is an integral part of the African way of life. Dance can be a form of entertainment and a way of worship, as well as a source or means of inspiration. In addition to these, there are as many reasons as there are dancers and dances. Like language, dance has similar manifestations of subjective feelings from the face-to-face issues in everyday life.

In Adwoa dance among the Akans of Ghana, there are elements of power and victory as well as fears. It is a dance that dramatizes the power of the Ashanti Kingdom. But underneath that could be warnings to their enemies against any intention to attack. One could suggest that the warnings may be precipitated by a deep sense of fear of how long their power will last. The same could be true for the annual Golog festival dance among the Tallensis and the Zulu war dance. When the Zulus enact that dance in Zululand, the dance can evoke powerful emotions of victory and fear that may have been passed on to the present generations.

There are two advantages of the dance that may be used for therapy. It may be viewed as an activity that may be detached from the historical setting but evokes one's emotions and energies to foster healing. If these emotions were not released, they could be destructive or might already be destroying the individual and community.

For the Tallensis, the Akans, and the Zulus, the dances may serve as a form of community therapy. Anyone who has watched the Zulu war dance could pick up in the enactments some anxiety and the powerful emotions associated with the anxiety. To put it psychologically, these different types of dances may be objectifying the individual feelings of anxiety caused by fears of insecurity. Dance as a bodily expression does have a therapeutic "character of an objectively available sign."[1]

One could see here the undifferentiatedness of the African world in dance more than perhaps in other aspects of life. Dance may serve as a form of abandonment of "emotions and controlled behavior, of social life, and the expression of individuality, of play, religion, battle, and drama."[2] Sachs puts it beautifully when he says that in dance, "repressed powers are loosed and seek expression. [The dancer] in ecstasy...bridges the chasm between this and the other world, to the realm of spirits and God."[3] For

Sachs, the dance "inherited from the ancestors as an ordered expression in motion of the exhilaration of the soul, develops and broadens into a search for God, into a conscious effort to become a part of those powers beyond the might of one, who controls our destinies."[4]

In the case of dance associated with death, the dance could become "a sacrificial rite, a charm, a prayer, and a prophetic vision. It summons and dispels the forces of nature, heals the sick, links the dead to the chain of descendants; it assures sustenance,...victory in battle,...blesses field and tribe."[5] One could suggest that in dance, there is an interplay of what Freud calls the eros and the death (thanatos) instincts.

In dance, aggression may also be acted out. However, aggression is not used here in a destructive sense, but rather as an initiative urge that brings forth creativity, the potential to transcend apparent limits. This notion may be more important if the history of the evolution of these communities is taken seriously. They may have had to survive through odds. So in Adwoa, the dancer among the Akans shakes a fist to symbolize strength and he/she crosses his/her two index fingers to symbolize unity.

Unfortunately, not many western scholars seemed to understand the constructive use of aggression by Africans. For example, Leo Frobenius and Douglas Fox who explore aggression in their book African Genesis,[6] seem to make inappropriate comparisons. They observe animals such as rats and conclude that the principle underlying aggression in Africans is due to a territorial imperative.

This notion came out of observation of the different types of behavior of rats. As a criticism of applying behavior of rats to humans, a similar analogy was stretched to apply to territorial conflicts of Germans and English Europeans. The answer of Frobenius and Fox was that rats cannot be compared with humans. In like manner, Africans can demand that Frobenius and Fox not equate behavior of rats to Africans. Theories of this nature may have been influenced by social Darwinism.

Dancing as psychological aggression could be seen as helping some Africans to a high degree of creativity. In others it could be a form of displacement. Freud introduced the word "displacement" to refer to a way of shifting an effect and its behavioral agents from the original source to a substitute.[7] As a theory, the substitute must resemble the original in some way in order not to create a perceptive or

118

cognitive problem. The advantage is that there could be a relief from frustration, and consequently, danger of destruction may be averted.

Another idea that may be of value for pastoral counseling is the notion of catharsis. Catharsis by definition means to make clean. It is argued as above that when aggression occurs, it releases the energy that has been built up. The place of catharsis "is the purging of such a drive or energy and the cathartic effect is the subsequent lessening of the arousability in the face of frustration and aggressive tendency."[8]

In dances such as the Golog dance of the Tallensis and the Zulu war dance, these Africans try to give a new sense of direction to their lives. They re-enact their experiences together in meaningful ways. At times, it may be in these dances that the unity of life is most effectively achieved. Some of these dances may also be their attempt to remove any barriers that exist among themselves, that is, the intrapsychical barriers as well as the interpersonal barriers. These barriers may be removed by acting out implicitly but effectively their feelings for each other.

Through dance, life may be shared, because the dancers allow each other to participate in each other's lives.[9] Kirk, in discussing the significance of dance in Mexico, echoes insights that could be true of some African dances. She writes:

> Dance assists us to envision as an event of dialogue where the subject matter takes over and we are lost in the happening. To live humanly is to be in conversation with others. The dialogue of dance takes place in community and dance arises out of community because all conversation is collaborative.[10]

One cannot help but agree with Kirk that by extension in some African communities dance

> is [their] paradigm for understanding what it means to be a human: to have a communal and carnal existence. ... dance puts us in touch with our stories, shared life and our ties to the earth. It is a new way of seeing by means of imagination.[11]

Implication For Counseling

Dance, as briefly discussed so far, offers an African pastoral counselor a helpful tool. How this is used will depend on the pastoral counselor, the counselee, and the context. So it is difficult to give any general theory that will be applicable to every situation. What follows are simply suggestions that may or may not be appropriate. They are offered to any pastoral counselor and counselee and their situation.

It is difficult to say whether or not dance is appropriate at the beginning, the middle, or the end of the counseling session. In some African communities, songs may be divided into categories.

These categories include songs of praise, victories, joy or lamentation, oppression, confessions, and intercession. These songs are in most cases accompanied by dances. Almost all events are accompanied by moods. Even when the events are forgotten, the moods may only be repressed but not forgotten if they were not appropriately integrated. In a session of counseling, an issue may be difficult to discuss.

It may be appropriate to ask the counselee to demonstrate in a dance to recapture his/her feelings. The counselor, in making this invitation, can expect anything and be open for anything. For example, a passive aggressive counselee under the hand of insensitive parents or spouse could explode with powerful repressed emotions that have been looking for ways to be expressed. A war dance may be appropriate and could be enacted on the scene.

One must also bear in mind that for some people dance may not be an appropriate way of reliving their story. A machoman, who believes a man should not weep or show emotions but must always appear to have everything together, no matter the circumstances, may not get up and dance at the beginning of a counseling session. For him to come to counseling could even be ego defeat. So the counselor should be sensitive. However, it will have been an effective help to this egomaniac, if at some stage of the session, the counselee could demonstrate in a dance what his (it's usually a man) inner world was or is like.

Dance may be most effective in group counseling especially group family counseling which may be more predominant in Africa, because of the strong family ties. These family ties at times may be hurting to other members. In family counseling, one could divide the family into groups and ask them to act out a war dance against each other. It may help the members of the family get insights into the dynamics of the conflicts among them. This may also help them open up to each other and develop a willingness to openly confront and do something about their problem. If they do, the family may have begun a journey to recapture family unity and solidarity, a vital necessity for survival of the family bond. Because dance and song do go together or evoke each other, an appropriate song will also be useful.

Perhaps dance may also be useful in exploring cases of witchery. In a case of witchery, it may be helpful to ask the victim or alleged victim and a relative to dramatize in a dance what circumstances led to bewitchery. The use of drama may recapitulate the emotions as well as the circumstances that have given cause to the accusation. Even if it happened months or even years ago, it may be possible to redramatize it. As stated earlier, emotions associated with some acts or events may be suppressed but not always eliminated. In addition to dramatizing witchery, dance and drama may further be helpful in explaining some mythological events, issues, beliefs and/or the residual elements of experiential encounters in sleep, on farms, traveling in the night, or in a service of worship in a Christian or traditional setting.

ENDNOTES

1.   Peter L. Berger and Thomas Luckman, The Social Construction of Reality: A Treatise In The Sociology of Knowledge, (Garden City, NY: Doubleday and Co., 1966), p. 36.

2.   Curt Sachs, World History of Dance, (New York: W.W. Norton, Inc., 1963), p. 3.

3.   Ibid., p. 4.

4.   Ibid.

5.   Ibid.

6.   Leo Frobenius and Douglas Fox, African Genesis, (New York: Stackpole Sons, 1937).

7.   Harry Kaufman, Aggression and Altruism, (New York: Holt, Rinehart and Winston, Inc., 1970), p. 30.

8.   Ibid.

9.   Martha Ann Kirk, Dancing with Creation, (Saratoga: California Resources Publication, Inc., 1978), p. 13.

10.   Ibid.

11.   Ibid., p. 14.

V. Music

Music is an integral part of life in Africa. It is used in many aspects of life, especially during transitions from one stage to another such as rites of birth, death, and marriage. Music is also used for entertainment as well as in religion. In most cases one involves the other, reflecting in the unitary concept of a person and life as a whole as discussed earlier. Music could be the way one witnesses the theory of the social construction of reality at its best. Music in Africa ranges from vocal to the snapping of fingers, tapping of the feet, and whistling. Instruments outside the body range from the use of two pieces of sticks to poetic talking drums such as those used by the Akans.[1]

Fela Sowande, in his discussion of the role of music in traditional African society, offers a helpful insight for the purpose of this chapter. He suggests that some forms of music, such as praise songs, are used "to reactivate and re-energize the psychic links which connect the human representatives with the psychic forces of which they are regents."[2]

Music is not just a skill one has acquired. Most people involved in music usually trace its roots to what Sowande calls a "patron deity" in the clan. The musician gets his/her inspiration from this patron deity. Perhaps Jung's notion of archetypes or primordial archetypes may offer a psychological insight in this respect, but this is not intended here.

As further suggested by Sowande, African music has a mythological origin and ministers to the psychosomatic needs of the group. It seems the equivalent of the psychosomatic needs alluded to here may be explored through the findings of psychophysiology. Pastoral counselors could tap the therapeutic values of the psychosomatic aspects of African music to enrich counseling with music in Africa.

One way African music meets psychosomatic needs may be by its ability to penetrate into "the personal-subjective feelings."[3] As rightly concluded by Euba, from an African perspective, "music is meaningful in its sociodramatic associations."[4] Duvelle makes helpful comment on music as an integral part of African life. He observes that "music is religion, work, entertainment,...closely linked to everyday life in traditional societies."[5] Music attempts to articulate and convey the experience of the community "in

123

rational and explicit language of its own [at times] ...as a therapeutic method."[6]

Most music in Africa corresponds to an occasion. That occasion may be a birth, death, initiation, coronation of king/queen, celebration of victories in war, disaster, anger, guilt, or helplessness. These could be both individual and corporate.

The music for any occasion depicts the mood of the occasion, hence accompanies or reflects the appropriate emotion. Many Africans can tell by the beat of a drum what occasion it is. The music not only reflects mood but in some cases dramatizes it. In the case of the talking drums of the Akans, the drums announce to the community what is happening or has happened. If the occasion is death, the drums, and the string instruments, may even eulogize, perhaps indicating the gifts of the dead or the occasion for the death.

There are special songs that enact the history or the identity of a group of people. For example, a song called lhubo is a very important song among members of a particular clan among the Zulu. Kriege suggests that "this song is treated with great respect by all members of the Sib and possesses a certain sentimentality of character."[7] According to Kriege, this song evokes memories of good times of peace and plenty to eat as well as a feeling of sadness implying feelings of fear and anxiety because of insecurity and not much to eat.

The people's history is re-enacted in this song. It objectifies the intrasubjectivity as well as intersubjectivity. Hence, singing such a song is not just entertainment but therapy as well.

Weman captured some of the essence of music in African culture when he said, "African music is intimately connected with African customs and practices. Where the ancient African culture lives on,...African music also lives on."[8] One can imagine the basic denial of African identity when the missionaries barred African Christians from using even traditional folk melodies with the Gospel message and their experiences. Experience here refers to their African spirituality as it was brought to bear on the Gospel of Jesus Christ. It may have been such frustration which led Gbeho to utter these words:

> I seriously attack the propagator of the idea that our music is primitive, fit only for the devil. [Western missionaries] have done many things of which I am justly proud, but their teachings...have done a lot to prohibit the music that is the center of our culture. The result is that today we have a

vast majority of educated Africans who have not the slightest idea of their own music and culture. Music being an important part of the culture of any nation, I therefore feel that to educate the African and leave out his music means that his education is lacking a foundation -- or in other words is but a thin veneer.9

The author shares the frustration of Gbeho's anger, and feels it is possible to integrate at least some parts of the African music with the Christian message.

The significance of African music, African experiences, cannot be over-emphasized. Music gives Africans a tool to appropriate meaning in their lives; it enables them not only to survive the hardships of life, but also to dramatize those hardships with hope and aspiration.

In religon, it is their music that offers them a way of grasping the divine in their search for meaning of life and their place in the world, as well as strength to rise above the odds. Music offers them a means to reconcile with each other and support each other. Music therefore can be an inevitable source for any authentic mode of counseling.

Music, like dance, can make an immense contribution to counseling in Africa. As indicated earlier, most songs in Africa can be classified into some basic categories. These categories include songs of praises, of victories, of joy, or of lamentation over being a victim under oppression of confession -- of intercession.

All songs that fall directly under any of these categories are usually accompanied by some strong emotion of one kind or another. Some are even born out of a particular historical circumstance. In such a case, singing the song may not just be entertainment but may recapitulate an historical experience precipitating stong emotions. If one visits an African house, it may be possible to deduce what may have immediately transpired in the family if one listens to the songs usually sung by the women. At times, the song may reflect the immediate circumstances between husband and wife, but it could be a circumstance between the family as a unit against another of the same clan or even the whole family against another family.

This practice even exists among Christians in African Churches. A particular song or hymn from the church hymnal does at times reflect the living experiences of an individual or family, hence it becomes a family favorite. It is not uncommon to see people weeping or in ecstasy while singing a particular song.

The reason behind these emotions is hard to understand for an outsider but certainly means a great deal to the one concerned.

Implication for Counseling

As with dance, what is suggested here are not universal rules. One way music can be used in counseling could be at the beginning of the session. When the anxiety and the defenses of the counselee are high and the counselor at times is at a loss to know what enhances rapport or destroys it, a song of association rather than words of association may be helpful for some Africans.

This approach may be more helpful especially for those rural people who are not afraid to show their emotions or may not have much to hide. Song association or just singing a favorite that tells his/her story may be an important counseling encounter from which the various pieces of the counselee's concerns can be brought into focus.

Music could also be used in counseling where the song could be a means of channeling emotions which are otherwise choked. The song may lead to weeping and/or laughing. The emotions may reflect the hurt of the circumstances which, when repressed, may prevent wholeness or health or, better put, shalom.

Merriam is quoted by Radocy and Boyle to have developed helpful contributions of music for therapy. According to Radocy and Boyle, Merriam made a distinction between uses and functions, which the author feels may be helpful. Uses refer to the contexts which provide opportune moments to appropriate the meaning of music. Functions of music, on the other hand, deal with the reasons, the general reasons why a particular piece of music is used. This distinction may be necessary for any counselor who wants to use music.

There may be different ways music could be used in counseling. Just to vary an approach suggested earlier, the counselor could start a session with a song and ask the patient to identify those parts of the song that have meanings for the counselee and then help explore why. The counselor could also at the end of the session suggest a song and use the same process of meaning or identifying its relevance with regard to insights made by the patient. If this approach is carefully used at the end, it may

126

help the counselee come out of the session with some insights. However, one must be very careful using this approach. It seems susceptible to abuse by control and projection on the part of the counselor. Nonetheless, it could be an option.

It would be preferable for the counselee to choose a song either at the beginning, in the middle, or at the end of the session. The counselor would then help explore with the counselee its relevance to his/her problems, progress, or the lack thereof. As suggested by Radocy and Boyle, "music allows the release of otherwise inexpressible thoughts, ideas [feelings] and provides an opportunity to 'let off steam' with respect to...issues."[10] Music, as Radocy and Boyle observe, functions as "a symbolic representation of other things, ideas, and behaviors."[11]

According to Merriam, as paraphrased by Radocy and Boyle, music symbolizes on four levels: "(1) The symbolizing evident in song texts, (2) the symbolic reflection or affective or cultural meaning, (3) the reflection of other cultural behavior and values, and (4) the deep symbolism of universal principles."[12]

It may be appropriate for the counselor to bear these four levels in mind when using music. It may be possible for a particular song text to help the counselee make the identifications at these four levels. Generally, levels one to three seem the most common. The author feels that level four is for a counselor who probably is knowledgeable in literature and other cultural experiences to make the connections to universal symbols. One has in mind some of Jung's works on symbolism. Merriam may be right when she says "music in a sense is a summatory activity for the expression of values, a means whereby the heart of psychology of a culture is exposed."[13]

The function of music in levels one and two may be best described in the words of Gaston when he says, "music, then is a powerful expression of the interdependence of mankind, and from the lullaby to the funeral dirge, an expression of tender emotion."[14]

Lomax may be right from an African perspective that "music is man's vehicle for expressing what is most basic in his relationships with others."[15]

Emotions in music are more than just a physiological phenomenon. Listening to songs or music "of one's childhood or adolescence evokes feelings of childhood and adolescent experiences."[16] The view of Radocy and Boyle may be informative. It states that "the power of music to elicit strong feelings of experiences associated with it provides individuals [at times communities] with a mechanism for re-experiencing many significant events within their lives."[17] This may correspond to levels one, two, and three. The words of songs also have the potential to bring out some issues in the repressed but unconscious, forgotten feelings such as love, anger, hatred, etc. (level one).

Music does become therapeutic by direct associations. However, in some cases, music achieves this by indirect means. This is known as the intrasubjective experience. In intrasubjective experience, the person deduces some ideas, images instead of the direct images in the song. These derived images may have some therapeutic value in the life experience of the individual concerned. Such songs are symbols and not signs.

Music as a model for counseling in Africa can effectively help the individual at the intrapsychical level as well as integrate the individual into the community (interpersonal level).

The use of music in pastoral counseling as discussed so far is mostly concerned with the words of the songs. There is also another usage of music which is mostly concerned with melody, tone, harmony, timbre, and rhythm.

Music was used to treat different types of mental illness in ancient civilizations, and in American native Indian and other primary cultures all over the world.

In the Bible, King Saul is said to have been calmed from the torment of an evil spirit by music. When the evil spirit came on Saul, he would call David who would take his harp and play. Saul would be calmed and the evil spirit would leave him.

Among the Greeks, music played an important therapeutic part. Homer recounts that the flow of blood from the wound could cease by the songs of Autolyaus.[18]

Pythagoras, according to Porphyry, believed that some melodies and rhythms had therapeutic value in relation to human actions and motivations. The effect would be manifested in the tranquility of the soul. Indeed, he believed that music could cure diseases of body and mind.[19]

Plato thought of music as an effective form of therapy. In the Republic he writes, "Rhythm and harmony sink deep into the recesses of the soul and take the strongest hold there, bringing that grace of body and mind which is only to be found in one who is brought up in the right way."[20] These are but a few examples of the use of music therapy in the past.

The emphasis of the music therapy discussed here is concerned with rhythm, tone, melody, harmony, and timbre. Each will be considered with regard to its therapeutic function.

Rhythm/Beat

Most African Music may be characterized by the rhythm. It may be the rhythm or beat that caused people to name Black music, predominantly in America, "soul music." The music gets to one's "gut feelings." Rhythm is most intense and affects both body and bodily emotions. The rhythmic effect on the body may be only natural, for some aspects of the body function rhythmically; for example, the respiration, the heart beat, walking, and muscular movements. The rhythm of music can therefore influence the body by either inducing calm, peace, and harmony or chaos, anger, and frustration and uneasiness.

The rhythm of the music does not only influence the body but it may also influence the psychological and spiritual. The rhythms of joy, depression, strength and weakness, extraversion, and introversion have psychological impacts on the moods of the individual.[21]

Tone

Musical notes produce vibrations. These vibrations have both physical and psychological effects. The vibrations do affect different types of human emotions. However, it is difficult to ascribe an emotion to a particular musical note.[22]

Melody

Melodies are produced by the combination of rhythm, tones, and accents. Melodies tend to affect the unconscious and the superconscious most. According to Assagioli, melodies arouse not only emotions but also sensations, and images and urges, and they greatly influence the nervous system, respiration, and circulation -- all vital functions.

Harmony

The collective sounds of many tones at the same time produce harmony. Depending on the different rates of vibrations, a harmony or discord could be produced. Assagioli further suggests harmony has both physiological and psychological effects respectively. He is of the opinion that "the dissonances in modern music reflect the disunity; conflicts and crises that afflict modern man, tend with their suggestive influence to accentuate and exaggerate the evil."[24]

Timbre

Timbre refers to the special quality of sounds produced by different instruments. This special quality also solicits some emotional responses. These responses invariably have some powerful psychological effects.[25]

Implication
of the Use of Music in Counseling

One therapeutic function of music is compared to the function of sleep in the body. Music may offer the body rest which refreshes and calms the tensions and emotions. This may be most effective to people living in modern day cities in Africa. The daily stresses, mentally, physically and psychologically, are phenomenal in African cities.

A pastoral counselor may use music to induce relaxation as a more natural and less harmful alternative to chemical sedatives.

Music may also be used for those suffering from physical pain of one kind or another. This may prove to be more helpful than painkillers that may have side effects or may not be available to buy. Some people do not even have the money to buy those that are available. It could be more effective to use music for calming the elderly than chemical sedatives.

According to Assagioli, there are some people who either "have undeveloped or repressed emotional natures." This may make them "arid, dissatisfied, shut-up within themselves. To them music may give the magic touch which reawakens and warms the heart and restores communion with nature, humanity, and God."[26]

Music may also be used to motivate people to actions. Music in this case can make heroes of some inactive or timid people. It may also motivate them to a service of self in the reinforcement of the ego. There are some war songs that have the potential to perform this function in some African communities. The songs associated with the war dance of the Zulus and the Golog dance among the Tallensis are just a few examples. Music also "cheers and gladdens, smoothing the wrinkled foreheads, softening into smiles the hard lines of tightly closed lips."27

Music can also stimulate memory. It does this by its power for some access to the unconscious.

Music may also "facilitate intellectual activity and favour artistic and creative inspiration."28 Assagioli recounts the story of the Halian author Alfieri, who is said to have conceived all his tragedies either at the time he was listening to music or shortly after."29

Music may also have psychoanalytic use in counseling. As indicated earlier, music does influence the unconscious. It can enter into the unconscious. Consequently, it may reduce or overcome repressions and resistances and bring to the conscious some destructive emotions, drives, and complexes.30

Furthermore, music can also influence those impulses and render them less destructive by transforming them into healthy actions. This will enable these impulses "to contribute to the deepening of experience and the broadening and enriching of the personality."31

According to Assagioli, in order for music therapy to be effective, it should be applied according to some rules. Pastoral counselors may have to learn some helpful insights by observing some or all of these rules.

Assagioli bases these rules more on psychophysiological than aesthetic or artistic principles. Before a list of the rules can be made, there may be two conditions that must be observed in order to get the maximum effect.

The first condition is that the music must be adapted to the sociocultural context of the counselee.

The second condition could be that the music chosen have a specific character. This may help the music to induce the appropriate emotions and conditions necessary for healing in the counselee.

One must bear in mind the degree of subjectivity involved in these two conditions. One must be flexible and sensitive to the counselee's response and be ready to change. There are eight rules to be followed.

Rule One: Before one can begin with the music, the counselee has to have sufficient knowledge of the music. That knowledge must include its nature, structure and the effect expected. This may facilitate the counselee's awareness and readiness to appropriate the music. It may also be necessary for the counselee to be told the words of the music if illiterate; if literate, a copy of the music can be given to him/her to follow. With the words, one increases both the unconscious effect and conscious appropriation.

Rule Two: It may be better for the counselee to be in a relaxed mode during the music. This mode helps to "open the doors of the unconscious." One can cause the counselee to relax by different means and in different ways.

Rule Three: One must use the music for a certain amount of time. Preferably, it should be short, "to avoid fatigue and, therefore, induce defense reactions."[32]

Rule Four: It is usually helpful to repeat the piece of music. A.W. Ainlay, a physician, violinist, pianist, and composer offers some instructive observations with regard to the use of music. "It is quite astounding to see the good effects and relaxation that may be produced in certain types of neuropsychiatric patients by repeating soothing measures or phrases. The repetition seems to act like a gentle message if properly done."[33] This principle seems to be more suitable for Africans because in most African music, there is usually a chorus or refrain, which involves participation by the counselee.

Rule Five: The volume of the music must be well controlled. It may be better to work with a low volume. The reason for a low volume may be that "the desired effect is produced by the rhythm and other qualities previously mentioned (tone, melody, harmony, timbre) and not by the amount of sound which, when great, is apt to tire or jar the nervous system."[34]

Rule Six: For almost the same reason as in Rule Two, it may be most helpful if the counselee

132

rests for some time after the music. This may enhance the effect on the unconscious.

Rule Seven: Music can be used while the counselee is asleep. The reason is that the unconscious is both "active" and "receptive" during sleep. This may be most effective in some psychiatric cases.

Rule Eight: One has to be careful when choosing music for counseling. The choice of music may affect the quality of the whole session. So it must not be taken lightly.

From this brief presentation, it is obvious music may offer African counselors many opportunities to be effective in countless situations. Africa has much to offer; let us open our eyes, ears, and ourselves.

ENDNOTES

1.   J.H. Nketia, "The Contribution of African Culture to Christian Worship" in International Review of Mission, Vol. 47, No. 87, 1958.

2.   Chief Fela Sowande, "The Role of Music in Traditional African Society" in African Music Meeting in Yaounde (Cameroon) 23-27 February 1970, organized by UNESCO (UNESCO 1972), p. 64.

3.   Akin Euba, "Creative Potential and Propagation of African Traditional Music" in African Music (UNESCO 1972), p. 121.

4.   Ibid.

5.   Charles Duvelle, "Report on the Yaounde Meeting" in African Music (UNESCO 1972), p. 145.

6.   Ibid.

7.   E. Jensen Kriege, The Social System of the Zulus, (London: 1950), p. 339.

8.   Henry Weman, African Music and the Church in Africa, translated by Eric J. Sharpe, (Uppsala Appelberg Boktrycheria AB, 1960), p. 9.

9.   Philip Gbeho, "Music in the Gold Coast" in African Music Newsletter, 1954, p. 82.

10.   Rudolf E. Radocy and J. David Boyle, Psychological Foundations of Musical Behavior, (Springfield, Illinois: Charles C. Thomas Publishing Co., 1979), p. 165.

11.   Ibid., p. 166.

12.   Ibid.

13.   P.A. Merriam, The Anthropology of Music, (Chicago: Northwestern University Press, 1964), p. 225.

14.   E.T. Gaston, "Man and Music" in Music in Therapy, E.T. Gaston (ed.), (New York: MacMillan, 1968), p. 25.

15.   A. Lomax et. al., Folk Song Style in Culture, (Washington D.C.: American Association for Advancement of Science, 1968), p. 133.

16.   Radocy and Boyle (1979), p. 189.

17.   Ibid.

18.   Homer, Odyssey XIX, trans. Andrew, S.O., (New York: Dutton, 1953).

19.   Porphyry, De Vita Pythagorae Edit. A. Nanck (Leipzig: 1885).

20.   Plato, The Republic Book III, 401, Translated by F.M. Conford, (London: Oxford University Press, 1942), p. 88.

21.   Robert Assagioli, <u>Psychosynthesis</u>, (New York: Penguin Books, 1965), p. 240.

22.   Ibid.

23.   Ibid., p. 241.

24.   Ibid.

25.   Ibid.

26.   Ibid., p. 247.

27.   Ibid.

28.   Ibid., p. 248.

29.   Ibid.

30.   Ibid.

31.   Ibid.

32.   Ibid., p. 252.

33.   G.W. Ainlay "The Place of Music in Military Hospitals" in Dorothy M. Schullian and M. Schoen (eds) <u>Music and Medicine</u>, (New York: Schuman, 1948), p. 328.

34.   Assagioli, p. 253.

BIBLIOGRAPHY

Abroms, Gene M. "Persuasion In Psychotherapy" in The American Journal of Psychiatry. 124, 9, 1968.

Ackernecht, Erwin H. A Short History of Psychiatry. New York: Jafner Pub. Co. Inc., 1959.

Ainlay, G. W. "The Place of Music in Military Hospitals" in Dorothy M. Schullian and M. Schoen (eds) Music and Medicine. New York: Schuman, 1948.

Assagioli, Robert. Psychosynthesis. New York: Penguin Books, 1965.

Appiah-Kubi, Kofi. Man Cures, God Heals. New York: Friendship Press, 1981.

Assogiolli, Robert. Psychosynthesis. New York: Penguin Books, 1982.

Barbour, Ian G. Myths, Models and Paradigms. New York: Harper & Row Publisher, 1974.

Barker, W. H. and Sinclair, Cecilia. West African Folk TalesLondon: George A. Harrup & Co., 1917.

Bausch,William J. Story Telling: Imagination and Faith. Mystic, Connecticut: Twenty-third Publications, 1984.

Beier, Ulli, (ed.). The Origin of Life and Death - African Creation Myths. London: Heinemann, 1969.

Berger, Peter L. The Sacred Canopy. Garden City, N.Y.: Doubleday & Co., Inc., 1967.

Berger, Peter L. and Luckman, Thomas. The Social Construction of Reality: A Treatise in the Sociology of Knowledge. Garden City, N.Y.: Doubleday & Co., Inc., 1966.

Berinyuu, Abraham A. "A Transcultural Approach to Pastoral Care of the Sick" in Africa Theological Journal. vol. 16:1, 1987.

Berinyuu, Abraham A. "The Practice of Divination and Christian Pastoral Care and Counselling in Ghana." in Africa Christian Studies. vol. 3:3 Sept. 1987.

Berinyuu, Abraham A. Pastoral Care to the Sick in Africa. Frankfurt: Peter Lang, 1988.

Busia, K. A. "Has the Christian Faith Been Adequately Presented?" in International Review of Missionl. 50, 1961.

By Our Lifes -- Stories of Women Today and in the Bible. Geneva: W.C.C., 1985.

Capps, Donald. Life Cycle Theory and Pastoral Care, edited by Don Browning. Philadelphia: Fortress Press, 1983.

Clebsch, William A. and Jaekle, Charles R. Pastoral Care In Historical Perspective. Englewood Cliffs, N.J.: Prentice-Hall, 1964.

Crescimanno, Russel. Culture, Consciousness, and Beyond: An Introduction. New York: University Press of America, Inc., 1982.

Duvelle, Charles. "Report on the Yaounde Meeting" in African Music UNESCO 1972.

Emy, Pierre. The Child and its Environment in Black Africa, Translated, abridged and adapted by G. J. Wanjohl, Nairobi, Oxford University Press, 1981.

Euba, Akin. "Creative Potential and Propagation of African Traditional Music" in African Music UNESCO 1972.

Evans-Pritchard, E. E. Theories of Primitive Religion, Oxford: Clarendon Press, 1965.

Feldman, Susan. African Myths and Tales. New York: Dell Publishers Co., Inc., 1963.

Fine, Reuben. "Psychoanalysis" in Raymond Corsini's (ed) Current Psychotherapies. Itasca: F. E. Peacock Pub. Inc., 1973.

Fortes, Meyer. The Web of Clanship Among the Tallensis,. London: Oxford University Press, 1949.

Fortes, Meyer and Horton,Robin. Oedipus and Job in West Africa. London: Cambridge University Press, 1983.

Fox, Matthew (ed). Western Spirituality Historical Roots and Ecumenical Routes. Notre Dame: Fides Claretian, 1979.

Francis, Vida. "Gaps in Doctor-Patient Communication; Patient's Response to Medical Advice" in Psychosomatic Medicine, Current Journal Articles, compiled by J. Elizabeth Jeffress. Flushing N.Y.: Medical Examination Pub. Co., 1971.

Frank, Jerome D. Persuasion and Healing. New York: Schocken Books, 1964.

Freud, Sigmund. Character and Culture, New York: MacMillan Pub. Co. 1963.

Freud, Sigmund. Group Psychology and the Analysis of Ego, Authorized translation by James Strachey. New York: Liveright Pub. Co. 1951.

Freud,, Sigmund. Introductory Lectures on Psychoanalysis, translated by James Strachey. New York: W. W. Norton Co., 1966.

Freud, Sigmund. An Outline of Psycho-Analysis, translated by James Strachey. New York: W. W. Norton and Co., 1949.

Freud, Sigmund. Totem and Taboo. New York: Norton, 1952.

Frobenius, Leo and Fox, Douglas. African Genesis. New York: Stackpole Sons, 1937.

Gaston, E. T. "Man and Music" in Music in Therapy, E.T. Gaston (ed) New York: MacMillan, 1968.

Gbeho, Philip. "Music in the Gold Coast" in African Music Newsletter, 1954.

Geertz, Clifford. The Interpretation of Cultures. New York: Basic Books Inc., 1973.

Gluckman, Max. "Moral Crises: Magical and Secular Solutions" in Max Gluckman (ed) The Allocation of Responsibility. London: Manchester University Press, 1972.

Goody, Jack. Introduction in Meyer Fortes, Robin Horton (eds) Oedipus and Job in West Africa. Cambridge: Cambridge University Press, 1954.

GyeKye, Kwame. An Essay on African Philosophical Thought, Cambridge: Cambridge University Press, 1987.

Haley, Jay. Strategies of Psychotherapy. New York: Grune and Stratton, 1963.

Hillman, James. "A Note On Story" in Parabola. IV, 4, 1979.

Hiltner, Seward. Preface to Pastoral Theology. Nashville: Abingdon Press, 1985.

Hoffman,John C. Law, Freedom and Story: The Role Of Narrative In Therapy, Society And Faith. Waterloo, Canada: Wilfrid Laurier University Press, 1986.

Hogan, Robert. Personality Theory: The Personological Tradition. Englewood, N.J.: Prentice Hall, Inc., 1976.

Homer. Odyssey XIX, trans. Andrew, S.O. New York: Dutton, 1953.

Jung, Carl A., Von Franz, M. L., Henderson, Joseph L., Jacobi, Jolande, Jaffe, Ariele. Man and His Symbols. New York: Dell Publishing Co., Inc., 1968.

Kaufman, Harry. Aggression and Altruism. New York: Holt, Rinehart and Winston, Inc., 1970.

Kayode, J. O. Understanding African Traditional Religion, Ike-Ife Nigeria: University of Ife Press, 1984.

Kiev, Ari. Magic, Faith and Healing. New York: The Fortress, 1964.

King, Noel Q. African Cosmos: An Introduction to Religion in Africa. Belmont: Wadsworth Publishing Co. , 1986.

Kirk, Martha Ann. Dancing with Creation. Saratoga: California Resources Publication, Inc., 1978.

Knappert, Jan. Myth and Legends of Swahili. London: Heinemann Educational Books, 1970.

Kriege, E. Jensen. The Social System of the Zulus. London: 1950.

Kubie, L. S. "Review of Persuasion and Healing" in Journal of Nervous and Mental Diseases. 133, 1961.

Landy, Robert J. Drama Therapy: Concepts and Practices. Springfield, Ill.: Charles C. Thomas Publisher, 1986.

Lapsley, James N. "Practical Theology and Pastoral Care; an Essay in Pastoral Theology" in Don Browning (ed) Practical Theology. San Francisco: Harper and Row, 1983.

Lartey, Emmanuel Yartekwei. Pastoral Counselling in Inter-cultural Perspective. Frankfurt: Peter Lang, 1987.

Lomax, A., et. al. Folk Song Style in Culture. Washington D.C.: American Association for Advancement of Science, 1968.

MacIntyre, Alasdair. "Myth" in P. Edward (ed.) Encyclopedia of Philosophy. 5.

Malinowski, Bronislaw. Magic Science and Religion and Other Essays, Glencoe: The Free Press, 1948.

Mbiti, John. African Religion and Philosophy. London: Oxford University Press, 1969.

Mead, George H. "The Social Self", Journal of Philosophy Psychology and Scientific Method. 10, 1913.

Mead, George H. Mind, Self and Society. Chicago: University of Chicago Press, 1956.

Megil, Esther L. Education in the African Church. London: Geoffrey Chapman, 1981.

Mendonsa, Eugene L. Politics of Divination. Berkeley: University of California, 1982.

Merriam, P. A. The Anthropology of Music. Chicago: Northwestern University Press, 1964.

Metuh, Emefie Ikenge.   African Religions in Western Conceptual Schemes: The Problem of
      Interpretation. Gabe Pastoral Institute, 1985.

Meyerourtz, Eva L. R. The Akan of Ghana, London: Faber and Faber Ltd., 1958.

Mosala, Bernadette I. "Pastoral Care and Family Counselling: South African Experience" in Mosamba Ma
      Mpolo and Cecile De Sweemer (ed.) Families in Transition. Geneva: W.C.C., 1987.

Mpolo, Masamba Ma and Kalu, Wilheim (eds).   The Risk of Growth, Pastoral Counselling in Context.
      Geneva: WCC, 1985.

Nketia, J. H. "The Contribution of African Culture to Christian Worship" in International Review of Mission,
      47, 87, 1958.

Nkrumah, Kwame. Conscienism: Philosophy and Ideology for Decolonization and Development with
      Particular Reference to African Revolution. London: Publisher unknown, 1964.

Nwachukwu, Daisy N. "Perceptions of Family" in Masamba Ma Mpolo and Cecile De Sweener (Eds)
      Families in Transition. Geneva: WCC, 1987.

Obiego, Cosmas O Keche Kuo. African Image of Ultimate Reality. Frankfurt: Peter Lang, 1984.

Okorocha, Cyril C. The Meaning of Religious Conversion In Africa. Avebury: Gower Publishing Co. ,
      1987.

Parrinder, G. West African Psychology, London: Lutherworth Press, 1951.

Parrinder, Geoffrey. West African Religion. London: Epworth Press, 1949.

Plato. The Republic Book III, 401, Translated by F.M. Conford. London: Oxford University Press, 1942.

Porphyry. De Vita Pythagorae Edit. A. Nanck. Leipzig: 1885.

Radocy, Rudolph E. and Boyle, J. David.   Psychological Foundations of Musical Behavior. Springfield,
      Illinois: Charles C. Thomas Publishing Co., 1979.

Ray, Benjamin. African Religions. Englewood: Prentice-Hall, Inc., 1976.

Rief, P. Freud: The Mind of the Moralist. New York: Doubleday, 1959.

Ruch, E.A. and Anyanwu, K. C. African Philosophy. Rome: Catholic Book Agency --Officium Libri Catholici, 1984.

Sachs, Curt. World History of Dance. New York: W.W. Norton, Inc., 1963.

Schneiderman, Leo. The Psychology of Myth, Folklore and Religion. Chicago: Nelson-Hall, 1981.

Shorter, Aylward. African Christian Spirituality. London: Geoffrey Chapman, 1978.

Shorter, Aylward. "Recent Development in African Spirituality" in Edward Fashole-Luke, Richard Grey, Adrian Hasting, Edwin Tasie, Christianity in Independent Africa, Bloomington: Indiana University, 1978.

Smith, Edwin W. The Religion of the Lower Races. New York: the MacMillan Co. 1923.

Smith, W. Robertson. The Religion of the Semites. New York: 1957.

Sow, I. Anthropological Structures of Madness in Black Africa. New York: International Universities Press, 1980.

Sowande, Chief Fela. "The Role of Music in Traditional African Society" in African Music Meeting in Yaounde (Cameroon) 23-27 February 1970, organized by UNESCO 1972.

Sundkler, Bengt. The Christian Ministry in Africa. London: SCM Press, 1961.

Temple, Placide. Bantu Philosophy, translated by A. Rubbens. Paris: Presence Africane, 1959.

Temple, Placide . La Philosophie Bantoue. Paris: Presence Africain, 1948.

Thayer, Nelson S. T. Spirituality and Pastoral Care. Philadelphia: Fortress Press, 1985.

Turner, Victor W. Ndembu Divination. London: Manchester University Press, 1961.

Tyrrel, Bernard J. Christo-therapy II. New York: Paulist Press, 1982.

Wallace, Anthony F. C. Culture and Personality, New York: Random House, 1961/70.

Weman, Henry. African Music and the Church in Africa, translated by Eric J. Sharpe. Uppsala Appelberg Boktrycheria AB, 1960.

Winter, Gibson. Liberating Creation: Foundations of Religious Social Ethics. New York: Cross Road, 1981.

Wiredu, Kwasi. Philosophy and An African Culture, Cambridge: Cambridge University Press, 1980.

Zahan, Dominique. The Religion, Spirituality and Thought of Traditional Africans, translated by K. E. Martin and L. M. Martin. Chicago: University of Chicago Press, 1979.